courage.
100 verses
for your
daily journey.

Freeman-Smith, a division of Worthy Media, Inc.

134 Franklin Road, Suite 200, Brentwood, Tennessee 37027

The quoted ideas expressed in this book (but not Scripture verses) are not, in all cases, exact quotations, as some have been edited for clarity and brevity. In all cases, the author has attempted to maintain the speaker's original intent. In some cases, quoted material for this book was obtained from secondary sources, primarily print media. While every effort was made to ensure the accuracy of these sources, the accuracy cannot be guaranteed. For additions, deletions, corrections, or clarifications in future editions of this text, please write Freeman-Smith.

Scripture quotations are taken from:

The Holy Bible, King James Version (KJV)

The Holy Bible, New International Version (NIV) Copyright © 1973, 1978, 1984, by International Bible Society. Used by permission of Zondervan Publishing House. All rights reserved.

The Holy Bible, New King James Version (NKJV) Copyright © 1982 by Thomas Nelson, Inc. Used by permission.

Holy Bible, New Living Translation, (NLT) copyright © 1996. Used by permission of Tyndale House Publishers, Inc., Wheaton, Illinois 60189. All rights reserved.

The Message (MSG)- This edition issued by contractual arrangement with NavPress, a division of The Navigators, U.S.A. Originally published by NavPress in English as THE MESSAGE: The Bible in Contemporary Language copyright 2002-2003 by Eugene Peterson. All rights reserved.

New Century Version®. (NCV) Copyright © 1987, 1988, 1991 by Word Publishing, a division of Thomas Nelson, Inc. All rights reserved. Used by permission.

The New American Standard Bible®, (NASB) Copyright © 1960, 1962, 1963, 1968, 1971, 1972, 1973, 1975, 1977, 1995 by The Lockman Foundation. Used by permission.

The Holman Christian Standard Bible™ (HCSB) Copyright © 1999, 2000, 2001 by Holman Bible Publishers. Used by permission.

Cover Design by Kim Russell / Wahoo Designs
Page Layout by Bart Dawson

ISBN 978-1-60587-351-0

Printed in the United States of America

courage.

100 verses
for your
daily journey.

Introduction

There are some Bible verses that are so important, so crucial to the Christian faith, that every believer should consider them carefully and review them often. This text examines 100 of the most familiar verses from God's Holy Word. These verses, which you've probably heard many times before, are short enough, and memorable enough, to provide courage for your daily journey. So do yourself and your loved ones a favor: study each verse and do your best to place it permanently in your mind and in your heart. When you do, you'll discover that having God's Word in your heart is even better than having a Bible on your bookshelf.

For God so loved the world, that he gave his only begotten Son, that whosoever believeth in him should not perish, but have everlasting life.

John 3:16 KJV

The Gift of Eternal Life

We begin with John 3:16, a verse that you've undoubtedly known since childhood. After all, this verse is, quite possibly, the most widely recognized sentence in the entire Bible. But even if you memorized this verse many years ago, you still need to make sure it's a verse that you can recite by heart.

John 3:16 makes this promise: If you believe in Jesus, you will live forever with Him in heaven. It's an amazing promise, and it's the cornerstone of the Christian faith.

Eternal life is not an event that begins when you die. Eternal life begins when you invite Jesus into your heart right here on earth. So it's important to remember that God's plans for you are not limited to the ups and downs of everyday life. If you've allowed Jesus to reign over your heart, you've already begun your eternal journey.

As mere mortals, our vision for the future, like our lives here on earth, is limited. God's vision is not burdened by such limitations: His plans extend throughout all eternity.

Let us praise the Creator for His priceless gift, and let us share the Good News with all who cross our paths. We return our Father's love by accepting His grace and by sharing His message and His love. When we do, we are blessed here on earth and throughout all eternity.

Let us see the victorious Jesus,
the conqueror of the tomb,
the one who defied death.
And let us be reminded that we, too,
will be granted the same victory.

—

Max Lucado

More Great Ideas About Eternal Life

Your choice to either receive or reject the Lord Jesus Christ will determine where you spend eternity.

Anne Graham Lotz

If you are a believer, your judgment will not determine your eternal destiny. Christ's finished work on Calvary was applied to you the moment you accepted Christ as Savior.

Beth Moore

I can still hardly believe it. I, with shriveled, bent fingers, atrophied muscles, gnarled knees, and no feeling from the shoulders down, will one day have a new body— light, bright and clothed in righteousness—powerful and dazzling.

Joni Eareckson Tada

God's salvation comes as a gift; it is eternal, and it is a continuum, meaning it starts when I receive the gift in faith and is never-ending.

Franklin Graham

All that is not eternal is eternally out of date.

C. S. Lewis

Be strong and courageous, and do the work. Don't be afraid or discouraged, for the Lord God, my God, is with you. He won't leave you or forsake you.

1 Chronicles 28:20 HCSB

Courage for Today

Christians have every reason to live courageously. After all, the ultimate battle has already been won on the cross at Calvary. But even dedicated followers of Christ may find their courage tested by the inevitable disappointments and fears that visit the lives of believers and non-believers alike.

When you find yourself worried about the challenges of today or the uncertainties of tomorrow, you must ask yourself whether or not you are ready to place your concerns and your life in God's all-powerful, all-knowing, all-loving hands. If the answer to that question is yes—as it should be—then you can draw courage today from the source of strength that never fails: your Heavenly Father.

More Great Ideas About Courage

The truth of Christ brings assurance and so removes the former problem of fear and uncertainty.

A. W. Tozer

If a person fears God, he or she has no reason to fear anything else. On the other hand, if a person does not fear God, then fear becomes a way of life.

Beth Moore

Courage is contagious.

Billy Graham

Daniel looked into the face of God and would not fear the face of a lion.

C. H. Spurgeon

Our Lord is searching for people who will make a difference. Christians dare not dissolve into the background or blend into the neutral scenery of the world.

Charles Swindoll

Courage is not simply one of the virtues, but the form of every virtue at the testing point, which means, at the point of highest reality. A chastity or honesty or mercy which yields to danger will be chaste or honest or merciful only on conditions. Pilate was merciful till it became risky.

C. S. Lewis

With each new experience of letting God be in control, we gain courage and reinforcement for daring to do it again and again.

Gloria Gaither

When once we are assured that God is good, then there can be nothing left to fear.

Hannah Whitall Smith

Are you fearful? First, bow your head and pray for God's strength. Then, raise your head knowing that, together, you and God can handle whatever comes your way.

Jim Gallery

There comes a time when we simply have to face the challenges in our lives and stop backing down.

John Eldredge

This is the day which the LORD hath made; we will rejoice and be glad in it.

Psalm 118:24 KJV

Celebrate the Gift of Life

Today is a non-renewable resource—once it's gone, it's gone forever. Our responsibility, as thoughtful believers, is to use this day in the service of God's will and in the service of His people. When we do so, we enrich our own lives and the lives of those whom we love.

God has richly blessed us, and He wants you to rejoice in His gifts. That's why this day—and each day that follows—should be a time of prayer and celebration as we consider the Good News of God's free gift: salvation through Jesus Christ.

Oswald Chambers correctly observed, "Joy is the great note all throughout the Bible." E. Stanley Jones echoed that thought when he wrote, "Christ and joy go together." But, even the most dedicated Christians can, on occasion, forget to celebrate each day for what it is: a priceless gift from God.

What do you expect from the day ahead? Are you expecting God to do wonderful things, or are you living beneath a cloud of apprehension and doubt? The familiar words of Psalm 118:24 remind us that every day is a cause for celebration. Our duty, as believers, is to rejoice in God's marvelous creation.

Today, celebrate the life that God has given you. Today, put a smile on your face, kind words on your lips, and a song in your heart. Be generous with your praise and free with your encouragement. And then, when you have celebrated life to the fullest, invite your friends to do likewise. After all, this is God's day, and He has given us clear instructions for its use. We are commanded to rejoice and be glad. So, with no further ado, let the celebration begin…

Now is the only time worth having
because, indeed, it is
the only time we have.

—

C. H. Spurgeon

More Great Ideas About
Joyful Living

When we truly walk with God throughout our day, life slowly starts to fall into place.

Bill Hybels

If you can forgive the person you were, accept the person you are, and believe in the person you will become, you are headed for joy. So celebrate your life.

Barbara Johnson

When the dream of our heart is one that God has planted there, a strange happiness flows into us. At that moment, all of the spiritual resources of the universe are released to help us. Our praying is then at one with the will of God and becomes a channel for the Creator's purposes for us and our world.

Catherine Marshall

As Christians, we must live a day at a time. No person, no matter how wealthy or gifted, can live two days at a time. God provides for us day by day.

Warren Wiersbe

*But those who wait on the Lord shall renew their strength;
they shall mount up with wings like eagles, they shall run and
not be weary, they shall walk and not faint.*

Isaiah 40:31 NKJV

Strength from God

Even the most inspired Christians can, from time
to time, find themselves running on empty. The
demands of daily life can drain us of our strength
and rob us of the joy that is rightfully ours in Christ.
When we find ourselves tired, discouraged, or worse,
there is a source from which we can draw the power
needed to recharge our spiritual batteries. That source
is God.

God intends that His children lead joyous lives
filled with abundance and peace. But sometimes, abundance and peace seem very far away. It is then that we
must turn to God for renewal, and when we do, He will
restore us if we allow Him to do so.

Today, like every other day, is literally brimming
with possibilities. Whether we realize it or not, God is
always working in us and through us; our job is to let
Him do His work without undue interference. Yet we
are imperfect beings who, because of our limited vision,

often resist God's will. And oftentimes, because of our stubborn insistence on squeezing too many activities into a 24-hour day, we allow ourselves to become exhausted, or frustrated, or both.

Are you tired or troubled? Turn your heart toward God in prayer. Are you weak or worried? Take the time— or, more accurately, make the time—to delve deeply into God's Holy Word. Are you spiritually depleted? Call upon fellow believers to support you, and call upon Christ to renew your spirit and your life. Are you simply overwhelmed by the demands of the day? Pray for the wisdom to simplify your life. Are you exhausted? Pray for the wisdom to rest a little more and worry a little less.

When you do these things, you'll discover that the Creator of the universe stands always ready and always able to create a new sense of wonderment and joy in you.

We have a God who delights
in impossibilities.

—

Andrew Murray

More Great Ideas About Strength

The same God who empowered Samson, Gideon, and Paul seeks to empower my life and your life, because God hasn't changed.

Bill Hybels

No matter how heavy the burden, daily strength is given, so I expect we need not give ourselves any concern as to what the outcome will be. We must simply go forward.

Annie Armstrong

When we spend time with Christ, He supplies us with strength and encourages us in the pursuit of His ways.

Elizabeth George

God conquers only what we yield to Him. Yet, when He does, and when our surrender is complete, He fills us with a new strength that we could never have known by ourselves. His conquest is our victory!

Shirley Dobson

A divine strength is given to those who yield themselves to the Father and obey what He tells them to do.

Warren Wiersbe

After this manner therefore pray ye: Our Father which art in heaven, Hallowed be thy name. Thy kingdom come. Thy will be done in earth, as it is in heaven. Give us this day our daily bread. And forgive us our debts, as we forgive our debtors. And lead us not into temptation, but deliver us from evil: For thine is the kingdom, and the power, and the glory, for ever. Amen

Matthew 6:9-13 KJV

The Lord's Prayer

"Our Father which art in heaven, hallowed be thy name." These familiar words begin the Lord's Prayer, a prayer that you've heard on countless occasions. It's the prayer that Jesus taught His followers to pray, and it's a prayer that you probably know by heart.

You already know what the prayer says, but have you thought carefully, and in detail, about exactly what those words mean? Hopefully so. After all, this simple prayer was authored by the Savior of mankind.

Today, take the time to carefully consider each word in this beautiful passage. When you weave the Lord's Prayer into the fabric of your life, you'll soon discover that God's Word and God's Son have the power to change everything, including you.

More Great Ideas About God

A sense of deity is inscribed on every heart.

John Calvin

I lived with Indians who made pots out of clay which they used for cooking. Nobody was interested in the pot. Everybody was interested in what was inside. The same clay taken out of the same riverbed, always made in the same design, nothing special about it. Well, I'm a clay pot, and let me not forget it. But, the excellency of the power is of God and not us.

Elisabeth Elliot

God is the beyond in the midst of our life.

Dietrich Bonhoeffer

God is not a supernatural interferer; God is the everlasting portion of his people. When a man born from above begins his new life, he meets God at every turn, hears him in every sound, sleeps at his feet, and wakes to find him there.

Oswald Chambers

It takes all time and eternity to know God.

Oswald Chambers

God has put into each of our lives a void that cannot be filled by the world. We may leave God or put Him on hold, but He is always there, patiently waiting for us . . . to turn back to Him.

Emilie Barnes

When all else is gone, God is left, and nothing changes Him.

Hannah Whitall Smith

God is an infinite circle whose center is everywhere and whose circumference is nowhere.

St. Augustine

The God who dwells in heaven is willing to dwell also in the heart of the humble believer.

Warren Wiersbe

The Lord is my shepherd; I shall not want. He makes me to lie down in green pastures; He leads me beside the still waters. He restores my soul.

Psalm 23:1-3 NKJV

God's Protection

D avid, the author of the 23rd Psalm, realized that God was his shield, his protector, and his salvation. And if we're wise, we realize it, too. After all, God has promised to protect us, and He intends to keep His promise.

In a world filled with dangers and temptations, God is the ultimate armor. In a world filled with misleading messages, God's Word is the ultimate truth. In a world filled with more frustrations than we can count, God's Son offers the ultimate peace.

Will you accept God's peace and wear God's armor against the dangers of our world? Hopefully so—because when you do, you can live courageously, knowing that you possess the supreme protection: God's unfailing love for you.

The world offers no safety nets, but God does. He sent His only begotten Son to offer you the priceless gift of eternal life. And now you are challenged to return

God's love by obeying His commandments and honoring His Son.

Sometimes, in the crush of everyday life, God may seem far away, but He is not. God is everywhere you have ever been and everywhere you will ever go. He is with you night and day; He knows your thoughts and your prayers. And, when you earnestly seek His protection, you will find it because He is here—always—waiting patiently for you to reach out to Him. And the next move, of course, is yours.

Prayer is our pathway not only to divine protection, but also to a personal, intimate relationship with God.

———

Shirley Dobson

More Great Ideas About God's Protection

Our responsibility is to feed from Him, to stay close to Him, to follow Him—because sheep easily go astray—so that we eternally experience the protection and companionship of our Great Shepherd the Lord Jesus Christ.

Franklin Graham

He goes before us, follows behind us, and hems us safe inside the realm of His protection.

Beth Moore

The Lord God of heaven and earth, the Almighty Creator of all things, He who holds the universe in His hand as though it were a very little thing, He is your Shepherd, and He has charged Himself with the care and keeping of you, as a shepherd is charged with the care and keeping of his sheep.

Hannah Whitall Smith

The Will of God will never take you where the Grace of God will not protect you.

Anonymous

Kept by His power—that is the only safety.

Oswald Chambers

But grow in the grace and knowledge of our Lord and Savior Jesus Christ. To Him be the glory both now and forever.

2 Peter 3:18 NKJV

Spiritual Growth

The words of 2 Peter 3:18 make it clear: spiritual growth is a journey, not a destination. When it comes to your faith, God doesn't intend for you to stand still; He wants you to keep moving and growing. In fact, God's plan for you includes a lifetime of prayer, praise, and spiritual growth.

Many of life's most important lessons are painful to learn. During times of heartbreak and hardship, we must be courageous and we must be patient, knowing that in His own time, God will heal us if we invite Him into our hearts.

Spiritual growth need not take place only in times of adversity. We must seek to grow in our knowledge and love of the Lord every day that we live. In those quiet moments when we open our hearts to God, the One who made us keeps remaking us. He gives us direction, perspective, wisdom, and courage. The appropriate moment to accept those spiritual gifts is the present one.

Are you as mature as you're ever going to be? Hopefully not! When it comes to your faith, God doesn't intend for you to become "fully grown," at least not in this lifetime. In fact, God still has important lessons that He intends to teach you. So ask yourself this: what lesson is God trying to teach me today? And then go about the business of learning it.

God's plan for our guidance is for us to grow gradually in wisdom before we get to the crossroads.

—

Bill Hybels

More Great Ideas About Spiritual Growth

If all struggles and sufferings were eliminated, the spirit would no more reach maturity than would the child.

Elisabeth Elliot

We look at our burdens and heavy loads, and we shrink from them. But, if we lift them and bind them about our hearts, they become wings, and on them we can rise and soar toward God.

Mrs. Charles E. Cowman

We set our eyes on the finish line, forgetting the past, and straining toward the mark of spiritual maturity and fruitfulness.

Vonette Bright

We are either the masters or the victims of our attitudes. It is a matter of personal choice. Who we are today is the result of choices we made yesterday. Tomorrow, we will become what we choose today. To change means to choose to change.

John Maxwell

A person who gazes and keeps on gazing at Jesus becomes like him in appearance.

E. Stanley Jones

Be still, and know that I am God....

Psalm 46:10 KJV

Be Still

We live in a noisy world, a world filled with distractions, frustrations, obligations, and complications. But we must not allow our clamorous world to separate us from God's peace. Instead, we must "be still" so that we might sense the presence of God.

If we are to maintain righteous minds and compassionate hearts, we must take time each day for prayer and for meditation. We must make ourselves still in the presence of our Creator. We must quiet our minds and our hearts so that we might sense God's love, God's will, and God's Son.

Has the busy pace of life robbed you of the peace that might otherwise be yours through Jesus Christ? If so, it's time to reorder your priorities. Nothing is more important than the time you spend with your Savior. So be still and claim the inner peace that is your spiritual birthright: the peace of Jesus Christ. It is offered freely; it has been paid for in full; it is yours for the asking. So ask. And then share.

More Great Ideas About Quiet Time

Since the quiet hour spent with God is the preacher's power-house, the devil centers his attention on that source of strength.

Vance Havner

The manifold rewards of a serious, consistent prayer life demonstrate clearly that time with our Lord should be our first priority.

Shirley Dobson

I don't see how any Christian can survive, let alone live life as more than a conqueror, apart from a quiet time alone with God.

Kay Arthur

That is the source of Jeremiah's living persistence, his creative constancy. He was up before the sun, listening to God's word. Rising early, he was quiet and attentive before his Lord. Long before the yelling started, the mocking, the complaining, there was this centering, discovering, exploring time with God.

Eugene Peterson

The Lord Jesus, available to people much of the time, left them, sometimes a great while before day, to go up to the hills where He could commune in solitude with His Father.

Elisabeth Elliot

In the center of a hurricane there is absolute quiet and peace. There is no safer place than in the center of the will of God.

Corrie ten Boom

When frustrations develop into problems that stress you out, the best way to cope is to stop, catch your breath, and do something for yourself, not out of selfishness, but out of wisdom.

Barbara Johnson

Quiet time is giving God your undivided attention for a predetermined amount of time for the purpose of talking to and hearing from Him.

Charles Stanley

Let this be your chief object in prayer, to realize the presence of your heavenly Father. Let your watchword be: Alone with God.

Andrew Murray

And now abide faith, hope, love, these three; but the greatest of these is love.

1 Corinthians 13:13 NKJV

The Greatest of These Is Love

The familiar words of 1st Corinthians 13 remind us of the importance of love. Faith is important, of course. So, too, is hope. But love is more important still.

Christ showed His love for us on the cross, and, as Christians, we are called upon to return Christ's love by sharing it. We are commanded (not advised, not encouraged...commanded!) to love one another just as Christ loved us (John 13:34). That's a tall order, but as Christians, we are obligated to follow it.

Sometimes love is easy (puppies and sleeping children come to mind) and sometimes love is hard (fallible human beings come to mind). But God's Word is clear: We are to love all our friends and neighbors, not just the lovable ones. So today, take time to spread Christ's message by word and by example. And the greatest of these is, of course, example.

More Great Ideas About Love

He who is filled with love is filled with God Himself.

St. Augustine

Those who abandon ship the first time it enters a storm miss the calm beyond. And the rougher the storms weathered together, the deeper and stronger real love grows.

Ruth Bell Graham

Love is an attribute of God. To love others is evidence of a genuine faith.

Kay Arthur

Love is the seed of all hope. It is the enticement to trust, to risk, to try, and to go on.

Gloria Gaither

It is when we come to the Lord in our nothingness, our powerlessness and our helplessness that He then enables us to love in a way which, without Him, would be absolutely impossible.

Elisabeth Elliot

32

How much a person loves someone is obvious by how much he is willing to sacrifice for that person.

Bill Bright

Live your lives in love, the same sort of love which Christ gives us, and which He perfectly expressed when He gave Himself as a sacrifice to God.

Corrie ten Boom

Suppose that I understand the Bible. And, suppose that I am the greatest preacher who ever lived! The Apostle Paul wrote that unless I have love, "I am nothing."

Billy Graham

Carve your name on hearts, not on marble.

C. H. Spurgeon

How do you spell love? When you reach the point where the happiness, security, and development of another person is as much of a driving force to you as your own happiness, security, and development, then you have a mature love. True love is spelled G-I-V-E. It is not based on what you can get, but rooted in what you can give to the other person.

Josh McDowell

But seek first the kingdom of God and His righteousness, and all these things shall be added to you. Therefore do not worry about tomorrow, for tomorrow will worry about its own things. Sufficient for the day is its own trouble.

Matthew 6:33-34 NKJV

Beyond Worry

Because we are imperfect human beings struggling with imperfect circumstances, we worry. Even though we, as Christians, have the assurance of salvation—even though we, as Christians, have the promise of God's love and protection—we find ourselves fretting over the inevitable frustrations of everyday life. Jesus understood our concerns when He spoke the reassuring words found in the 6th chapter of Matthew.

Where is the best place to take your worries? Take them to God. Take your troubles to Him; take your fears to Him; take your doubts to Him; take your weaknesses to Him; take your sorrows to Him . . . and leave them all there. Seek protection from the One who offers you eternal salvation; build your spiritual house upon the Rock that cannot be moved.

Perhaps you are concerned about your future, your health, or your finances. Or perhaps you are simply a "worrier" by nature. If so, make Matthew 6 a regular part of your daily Bible reading. This beautiful passage will remind you that God still sits in His heaven and you are His beloved child. Then, perhaps, you will worry a little less and trust God a little more, and that's as it should be because God is trustworthy . . . and you are protected.

Never yield to gloomy anticipation.
Place your hope and confidence in God.
He has no record of failure.

Mrs. Charles E. Cowman

More Great Ideas About Worry

The beginning of anxiety is the end of faith, and the beginning of true faith is the end of anxiety.

George Mueller

Worry is the senseless process of cluttering up tomorrow's opportunities with leftover problems from today.

Barbara Johnson

We are not called to be burden-bearers, but cross-bearers and light-bearers. We must cast our burdens on the Lord.

Corrie ten Boom

God is bigger than your problems. Whatever worries press upon you today, put them in God's hands and leave them there.

Billy Graham

Today is mine. Tomorrow is none of my business. If I peer anxiously into the fog of the future, I will strain my spiritual eyes so that I will not see clearly what is required of me now.

Elisabeth Elliot

Trust in the Lord with all your heart, and lean not on your own understanding; In all your ways acknowledge Him, and He shall direct your paths.

Proverbs 3:5-6 NKJV

Trust Him

I t's easy to talk about trusting God, but when it comes to actually trusting Him, that's considerably harder. Why? Because genuine trust in God requires more than words; it requires a willingness to follow God's lead and a willingness to obey His commandments. (These, by the way, are not easy things to do.)

Have you spent more time talking about Christ than walking in His footsteps? If so, God wants to have a little chat with you. And, if you're unwilling to talk to Him, He may take other actions in order to grab your attention.

Thankfully, whenever you're willing to talk with God, He's willing to listen. And, the instant that you decide to place Him squarely in the center of your life, He will respond to that decision with blessings that are too unexpected to predict and too numerous to count.

When you find your courage tested to the limit, lean upon God's promises. Trust His Son. Remember that God is always near and that He is your protector and your deliverer. When you are worried, anxious, or afraid, call upon Him. God can handle your troubles infinitely better than you can, so turn them over to Him. Remember that God rules both mountaintops and valleys—with limitless wisdom and love—now and forever.

Beware of trusting in yourself,
and see that you trust
in the Lord.

—

Oswald Chambers

More Great Ideas About Trusting God

God is God. He knows what he is doing. When you can't trace his hand, trust his heart.

Max Lucado

Sometimes the very essence of faith is trusting God in the midst of things He knows good and well we cannot comprehend.

Beth Moore

A prayerful heart and an obedient heart will learn, very slowly and not without sorrow, to stake everything on God Himself.

Elisabeth Elliot

Do not be afraid, then, that if you trust, or tell others to trust, the matter will end there. Trust is only the beginning and the continual foundation. When we trust Him, the Lord works, and His work is the important part of the whole matter.

Hannah Whitall Smith

Faith does not eliminate problems. Faith keeps you in a trusting relationship with God in the midst of your problems.

Henry Blackaby

I am the vine, you are the branches. He who abides in Me, and I in him, bears much fruit; for without Me you can do nothing.

John 15:5 NKJV

He Is the Vine

He was the Son of God, but He wore a crown of thorns. He was the Savior of mankind, yet He was put to death on a roughhewn cross. He offered His healing touch to an unsaved world, and yet the same hands that had healed the sick and raised the dead were pierced with nails.

Jesus Christ, the Son of God, was born into humble circumstances. He walked this earth, not as a ruler of men, but as the Savior of mankind. His crucifixion, a torturous punishment that was intended to end His life and His reign, instead became the pivotal event in the history of all humanity. Christ sacrificed His life on the cross so that we might have eternal life. This gift, freely given by God's only begotten Son, is the priceless possession of everyone who accepts Him as Lord and Savior.

Why did Christ endure the humiliation and torture of the cross? He did it for you. His love is as near as your next breath, as personal as your next thought, more essential than your next heartbeat. And what must you do in response to the Savior's gifts? You must accept His love, praise His name, and share His message of salvation. And, you must conduct yourself in a manner that demonstrates to all the world that your acquaintance with the Master is not a passing fancy but that it is, instead, the cornerstone and the touchstone of your life.

Sold for thirty pieces of silver, He redeemed the world.

—

R. G. Lee

More Great Ideas About Jesus

Jesus was the perfect reflection of God's nature in every situation He encountered during His time here on earth.

Bill Hybels

Jesus makes God visible. But that truth does not make Him somehow less than God. He is equally supreme with God.

Anne Graham Lotz

Tell me the story of Jesus. Write on my heart every word. Tell me the story most precious, sweetest that ever was heard.

Fanny Crosby

The crucial question for each of us is this: What do you think of Jesus, and do you yet have a personal acquaintance with Him?

Hannah Whitall Smith

Had Jesus been the Word become word, He would have spun theories about life, but since he was the Word become flesh, he put shoes on all his theories and made them walk.

E. Stanley Jones

Ask, and it will be given to you; seek, and you will find; knock, and it will be opened to you. For everyone who asks receives, and he who seeks finds, and to him who knocks it will be opened.

Matthew 7:7-8 NKJV

Ask Him for the Things You Need

How often do you ask God for His help and His wisdom? Occasionally? Intermittently? Whenever you experience a crisis? Hopefully not. Hopefully, you've acquired the habit of asking for God's assistance early and often. And hopefully, you have learned to seek His guidance in every aspect of your life.

In Matthew 7, God promises that He will guide you if you let Him. Your job is to let Him. But sometimes, you will be tempted to do otherwise. Sometimes, you'll be tempted to go along with the crowd; other times, you'll be tempted to do things your way, not God's way. When you feel those temptations, resist them.

God has promised that when you ask for His help, He will not withhold it. So ask. Ask Him to meet the needs of your day. Ask Him to lead you, to protect you, and to correct you. And trust the answers He gives.

God stands at the door and waits. When you knock, He opens. When you ask, He answers. Your task, of course, is to seek His guidance prayerfully, confidently, and often.

Some people think God does not like
to be troubled with our constant asking.
But, the way to trouble God
is not to come at all.

—

D. L. Moody

More Great Ideas About
Asking God

All we have to do is to acknowledge our need, move from self-sufficiency to dependence, and ask God to become our hiding place.

Bill Hybels

By asking in Jesus' name, we're making a request not only in His authority, but also for His interests and His benefit.

Shirley Dobson

When will we realize that we're not troubling God with our questions and concerns? His heart is open to hear us—his touch nearer than our next thought—as if no one in the world existed but us. Our very personal God wants to hear from us personally.

Gigi Graham Tchividjian

God uses our most stumbling, faltering faith-steps as the open door to His doing for us "more than we ask or think."

Catherine Marshall

God's help is always available, but it is only given to those who seek it.

Max Lucado

You shall have no other gods before Me.

Exodus 20:3 NKJV

Putting God First

Is God your top priority? Have you given His Son your heart, your soul, your talents, and your time? Or are you in the habit of giving God little more than a few hours on Sunday morning? The answers to these questions will determine how you prioritize your days and your life.

As you contemplate your own relationship with God, remember this: all of mankind is engaged in the practice of worship. Some people choose to worship God and, as a result, reap the joy that He intends for His children. Others distance themselves from God by worshiping such things as earthly possessions or personal gratification . . . and when they do so, they suffer.

In the book of Exodus, God warns that we should place no gods before Him. Yet all too often, we place our Lord in second, third, or fourth place as we worship the gods of pride, greed, power, or lust.

When we place our desires for material possessions above our love for God—or when we yield to temptations of the flesh—we find ourselves engaged in a struggle that is similar to the one Jesus faced when He was tempted by Satan. In the wilderness, Satan offered Jesus earthly power and unimaginable riches, but Jesus turned Satan away and chose instead to worship God. We must do likewise by putting God first and worshiping only Him.

Does God rule your heart? Make certain that the honest answer to this question is a resounding yes. In the life of every righteous believer, God comes first. That's precisely the place that He deserves in your heart, too.

You must never sacrifice your relationship with God for the sake of a relationship with another person.

—

Charles Stanley

More Great Ideas About Putting God First

Make God's will the focus of your life day by day. If you seek to please Him and Him alone, you'll find yourself satisfied with life.

Kay Arthur

It is impossible to please God doing things motivated by and produced by the flesh.

Bill Bright

A man's spiritual health is exactly proportional to his love for God.

C. S. Lewis

I love you, Lord, not doubtingly, but with absolute certainty. Your Word beat upon my heart until I fell in love with you, and now the universe and everything in it tells me to love you, and tells the same thing to us all.

St. Augustine

Jesus Christ is the first and last, author and finisher, beginning and end, alpha and omega, and by Him all other things hold together. He must be first or nothing. God never comes next!

Vance Havner

Cast thy burden upon the LORD, and he shall sustain thee: he shall never suffer the righteous to be moved.

Psalm 55:22 KJV

Casting Your Burdens

God's Word contains promises upon which we, as Christians, can and must depend. The Bible is a priceless gift, a tool that God intends for us to use in every aspect of our lives. Too many Christians, however, keep their spiritual tool kits tightly closed and out of sight.

Psalm 55:22 instructs us to cast our burdens upon the Lord. And that's perfect advice for men, women, and children alike.

Are you tired? Discouraged? Fearful? Be comforted and trust the promises that God has made to you. Are you worried or anxious? Be confident in God's power. He will never desert you. Do you see a difficult future ahead? Be courageous and call upon God. He will protect you and then use you according to His purposes. Are you confused? Listen to the quiet voice of your Heavenly Father. He is not a God of confusion. Talk with Him; listen to Him; trust Him, and trust His promises. He is steadfast, and He is your Protector . . . forever.

More Great Ideas About
God's Support

Faith is not merely you holding on to God—it is God holding on to you.

E. Stanley Jones

God uses our most stumbling, faltering faith-steps as the open door to His doing for us "more than we ask or think."

Catherine Marshall

God wants to reveal Himself as your heavenly Father. When you are hurting, you can run to Him and crawl up into His lap. When you wonder which way to turn, you can grasp His strong hand, and He'll guide you along life's path. When everything around you is falling apart, you'll feel your Father's arm around your shoulder to hold you together.

Lisa Whelchel

He stands fast as your rock, steadfast as your safeguard, sleepless as your watcher, valiant as your champion.

C. H. Spurgeon

Measure the size of the obstacles against the size of God.

Beth Moore

You will show me the path of life; in Your presence is fullness of joy; at Your right hand are pleasures forevermore.

Psalm 16:11 NKJV

He Will Show You the Path

L ife is best lived on purpose. And purpose, like everything else in the universe, begins in the heart of God. Whether you realize it or not, God has a direction for your life, a divine calling, a path along which He intends to lead you. When you welcome God into your heart and establish a genuine relationship with Him, He will begin—and He will continue—to make His purposes known.

Each morning, as the sun rises in the east, you welcome a new day, one that is filled to the brim with opportunities, with possibilities, and with God. As you contemplate God's blessings in your own life, you should prayerfully seek His guidance for the day ahead.

Discovering God's unfolding purpose for your life is a daily journey, a journey guided by the teachings of God's Holy Word. As you reflect upon God's promises and upon the meaning that those promises hold for you, ask God to lead you throughout the coming day. Let your Heavenly Father direct your steps; concentrate on what God wants you to do now, and leave the distant future in hands that are far more capable than your own: His hands.

Sometimes, God's intentions will be clear to you; other times, God's plan will seem uncertain at best. But even on those difficult days when you are unsure which way to turn, you must never lose sight of these overriding facts: God created you for a reason; He has important work for you to do; and He's waiting patiently for you to do it. So why not begin today?

The worst thing that laziness does
is rob a man of spiritual purpose.

—

Billy Graham

More Great Ideas About Living on Purpose

Continually restate to yourself what the purpose of your life is.

Oswald Chambers

His life is our light—our purpose and meaning and reason for living.

Anne Graham Lotz

Yesterday is just experience but tomorrow is glistening with purpose—and today is the channel leading from one to the other.

Barbara Johnson

Only God's chosen task for you will ultimately satisfy. Do not wait until it is too late to realize the privilege of serving Him in His chosen position for you.

Beth Moore

Without God, life has no purpose, and without purpose, life has no meaning.

Rick Warren

Now by this we know that we know Him, if we keep His commandments.

1 John 2:3 NKJV

Obedience Now

Obedience to God is determined, not by words, but by deeds. Talking about righteousness is easy; living righteously is far more difficult, especially in today's temptation-filled world.

Since God created Adam and Eve, we human beings have been rebelling against our Creator. Why? Because we are unwilling to trust God's Word, and we are unwilling to follow His commandments. God has given us a guidebook for righteous living called the Holy Bible. It contains thorough instructions which, if followed, lead to fulfillment, abundance, and salvation. But, if we choose to ignore God's commandments, the results are as predictable as they are tragic.

When we seek righteousness in our own lives—and when we seek the companionship of those who do likewise—we reap the spiritual rewards that God intends for our lives. When we behave ourselves as godly men and women, we honor God. When we live righteously and according to God's commandments, He blesses us in ways that we cannot fully understand.

Do you seek God's peace and His blessings? Then obey Him. When you're faced with a difficult choice or a powerful temptation, seek God's counsel and trust the counsel He gives. Invite God into your heart and live according to His commandments. When you do, you will be blessed today, and tomorrow, and forever.

God uses ordinary people
who are obedient to Him to do
extraordinary things.

—

John Maxwell

More Great Ideas About Obedience

Believe and do what God says. The life-changing consequences will be limitless, and the results will be confidence and peace of mind.

Franklin Graham

The cross that Jesus commands you and me to carry is the cross of submissive obedience to the will of God, even when His will includes suffering and hardship and things we don't want to do.

Anne Graham Lotz

You may not always see immediate results, but all God wants is your obedience and faithfulness.

Vonette Bright

Let us never suppose that obedience is impossible or that holiness is meant only for a select few. Our Shepherd leads us in paths of righteousness—not for our name's sake but for His.

Elisabeth Elliot

All Scripture is given by inspiration of God, and is profitable for doctrine, for reproof, for correction, for instruction in righteousness, that the man of God may be complete, thoroughly equipped for every good work.

2 Timothy 3:16-17 NKJV

The Use of Scripture

I s Bible study a high priority for you? The answer to this simple question will determine, to a surprising extent, the quality of your life and the direction of your faith.

As you establish priorities for life, you must decide whether God's Word will be a bright spotlight that guides your path every day or a tiny nightlight that occasionally flickers in the dark. The decision to study the Bible—or not—is yours and yours alone. But make no mistake: how you choose to use your Bible will have a profound impact on you and your loved ones.

George Mueller observed, "The vigor of our spiritual lives will be in exact proportion to the place held by the Bible in our lives and in our thoughts." The more you use your Bible, the more God will use you.

Perhaps you're one of those Christians who owns a bookshelf full of unread Bibles. If so, remember the old saying, "A Bible in the hand is worth two in the book-case." Or perhaps you're one of those folks who is simply "too busy" to find time for a daily dose of prayer and Bible study. If so, remember the old adage, "It's hard to stumble when you're on your knees."

God's Word can be a roadmap to a place of righteousness and abundance. Make it your roadmap. God's wisdom can be a light to guide your steps. Claim it as your light today, tomorrow, and every day of your life—and then walk confidently in the footsteps of God's only begotten Son.

It takes calm, thoughtful, prayerful meditation on the Word to extract its deepest nourishment.

—

Vance Havner

More Great Ideas About God's Word

The Holy Spirit is the Spirit of Truth, which means He always works according to and through the Word of God whether you feel Him or not.

Anne Graham Lotz

Either God's Word keeps you from sin, or sin keeps you from God's Word.

Corrie ten Boom

My meditation and study have shown me that, like God, His Word is holy, everlasting, absolutely true, powerful, personally fair, and never changing.

Bill Bright

God's Word is a light not only to our path but also to our thinking. Place it in your heart today, and you will never walk in darkness.

Joni Eareckson Tada

The Scriptures were not given for our information, but for our transformation.

D. L. Moody

I am come that they might have life, and that they might have it more abundantly.

John 10:10 KJV

Accepting God's Abundance

The 10th chapter of John tells us that Christ came to earth so that our lives might be filled with abundance. But what, exactly, did Jesus mean when He promised "life...more abundantly"? Was He referring to material possessions or financial wealth? Hardly. Jesus offers a different kind of abundance: a spiritual richness that extends beyond the temporal boundaries of this world.

Is material abundance part of God's plan for our lives? Perhaps. But in every circumstance of life, during times of wealth or times of want, God will provide us with what we need if we trust Him (Matthew 6). May we, as believers, claim the riches of Christ Jesus every day that we live, and may we share His blessings with all who cross our path.

More Great Ideas About Abundance

God loves you and wants you to experience peace and life—abundant and eternal.

Billy Graham

The gift of God is eternal life, spiritual life, abundant life through faith in Jesus Christ, the Living Word of God.

Anne Graham Lotz

God's riches are beyond anything we could ask or even dare to imagine! If my life gets gooey and stale, I have no excuse.

Barbara Johnson

Yes, we were created for His holy pleasure, but we will ultimately—if not immediately—find much pleasure in His pleasure.

Beth Moore

The only way you can experience abundant life is to surrender your plans to Him.

Charles Stanley

It would be wrong to have a "poverty complex," for to think ourselves paupers is to deny either the King's riches or to deny our being His children.

Catherine Marshall

Jesus intended for us to be overwhelmed by the blessings of regular days. He said it was the reason he had come: "I am come that they might have life, and that they might have it more abundantly."

Gloria Gaither

Jesus wants Life for us, Life with a capital L.

John Eldredge

The Bible says that being a Christian is not only a great way to die, but it's also the best way to live.

Bill Hybels

People, places, and things were never meant to give us life. God alone is the author of a fulfilling life.

Gary Smalley & John Trent

Now may the God of hope fill you with all joy and peace in believing, so that you may overflow with hope by the power of the Holy Spirit.

Romans 15:13 HCSB

Big Dreams

Are you willing to entertain the possibility that God has big plans in store for you? Hopefully so. Yet sometimes, especially if you've recently experienced a life-altering disappointment, you may find it difficult to envision a brighter future for yourself and your family. If so, it's time to reconsider your own capabilities . . . and God's.

Your Heavenly Father created you with unique gifts and untapped talents; your job is to tap them. When you do, you'll begin to feel an increasing sense of confidence in yourself and in your future.

It takes courage to dream big dreams. You will discover that courage when you do three things: accept the past, trust God to handle the future, and make the most of the time He has given you today.

Nothing is too difficult for God, and no dreams are too big for Him—not even yours. So start living—and dreaming—accordingly.

More Great Ideas About Dreams

You cannot out-dream God.

John Eldredge

To make your dream come true, you have to stay awake.

Dennis Swanberg

The future lies all before us. Shall it only be a slight advance upon what we usually do? Ought it not to be a bound, a leap forward to altitudes of endeavor and success undreamed of before?

Annie Armstrong

Sometimes our dreams were so big that it took two people to dream them.

Marie T. Freeman

Always stay connected to people and seek out things that bring you joy. Dream with abandon. Pray confidently.

Barbara Johnson

Set goals so big that unless God helps you, you will be a miserable failure.

Bill Bright

But each person should examine his own work, and then he will have a reason for boasting in himself alone, and not in respect to someone else. For each person will have to carry his own load.

Galatians 6:4-5 HCSB

Your Duties to Him

Nobody needs to tell you the obvious: You have lots of responsibilities—obligations to yourself, to your family, to your community, and to your God. And which of these duties should take priority? The answer can be found in Matthew 6:33: "But seek first the kingdom of God and His righteousness, and all these things will be provided for you" (HCSB).

When you "seek first the kingdom of God," all your other obligations have a way of falling into place. When you obey God's Word and seek His will, your many responsibilities don't seem quite so burdensome. When you honor God with your time, your talents. and your prayers, you'll be much more likely to count your blessings instead of your troubles. So do yourself and your loved ones a favor: take all your duties seriously, especially your duties to God.

More Great Ideas About Duty

If you seek to know the path of your duty, use God as your compass.

C. H. Spurgeon

There is an active practice of holiness as we carry out, for the glory of God, the ordinary duties of each day, faithfully fulfilling the responsibilities given us. The passive practice consists in loving acceptance of the unexpected, be it welcome or unwelcome, remembering that we have a wise and sovereign Lord who works in mysterious ways and is never taken by surprise.

Elisabeth Elliot

When the law of God is written on our hearts, our duty will be our delight.

Matthew Henry

The secret of a happy life is to delight in duty. When duty becomes delight, then burdens become blessings.

Warren Wiersbe

The secret of a happy life is to do your duty and trust in God.

Sam Jones

For this very reason, make every effort to supplement your faith with goodness, goodness with knowledge, knowledge with self-control, self-control with endurance, endurance with godliness.

2 Peter 1:5-6 HCSB

Rising Above Those Negative Emotions

Over and over again, the Bible instructs us to live by faith. Yet sometimes, despite our best intentions, negative feelings can rob us of the peace and abundance that would otherwise be ours through Christ. When anger or anxiety separates us from the spiritual blessings that God has in store, we must rethink our priorities. And we must place faith above feelings.

Human emotions are highly variable, decidedly unpredictable, and often unreliable. Our emotions are like the weather, only sometimes far more fickle. So we must learn to live by faith, not by the ups and downs of our own emotional roller coasters.

Sometime during the coming day, you may encounter a tough situation or a difficult person. And as a result, you may be gripped by a strong negative emotion. Distrust it. Reign it in. Test it. And turn it over to God.

Your emotions will inevitably change; God will not. So trust Him completely. When you do, you'll be surprised at how quickly those negative feelings can evaporate into thin air.

More Great Ideas About Emotions

Wisdom always waits for the right time to act, while emotion always pushes for action right now.

Joyce Meyer

I may no longer depend on pleasant impulses to bring me before the Lord. I must rather respond to principles I know to be right, whether I feel them to be enjoyable or not.

Jim Elliot

If you are going to be a person who is committed to the Word of God, you will have to learn to be led by the Spirit and not by your emotions.

Joyce Meyer

The only serious mistake we can make is the mistake that Psalm 121 prevents: the mistake of supposing that God's interest in us waxes and wanes in response to our spiritual temperature.

Eugene Peterson

But encourage each other daily, while it is still called today, so that none of you is hardened by sin's deception.

Hebrews 3:13 HCSB

The Power of Encouragement

Life is a team sport, and all of us need occasional pats on the back from our teammates. As Christians, we are called upon to spread the Good News of Christ, and we are also called to spread a message of encouragement and hope to the world.

Whether you realize it or not, many people with whom you come in contact every day are in desperate need of a smile or an encouraging word. The world can be a difficult place, and countless friends and family members may be troubled by the challenges of everyday life. Since you don't always know who needs your help, the best strategy is to try to encourage all the people who cross your path. So today, be a world-class source of encouragement to everyone you meet. Never has the need been greater.

More Great Ideas About Encouragement

Make it a rule, and pray to God to help you to keep it, never to lie down at night without being able to say: "I have made at least one human being a little wiser, a little happier, or a little better this day."

Charles Kingsley

God grant that we may not hinder those who are battling their way slowly into the light.

Oswald Chambers

I can usually sense that a leading is from the Holy Spirit when it calls me to humble myself, to serve somebody, to encourage somebody, or to give something away. Very rarely will the evil one lead us to do those kind of things.

Bill Hybels

God is still in the process of dispensing gifts, and He uses ordinary individuals like us to develop those gifts in other people.

Howard Hendricks

He climbs highest who helps another up.

Zig Ziglar

No journey is complete that does not lead through some dark valleys. We can properly comfort others only with the comfort we ourselves have been given by God.

Vance Havner

God of our life, there are days when the burdens we carry chafe our shoulders and weigh us down; when the road seems dreary and endless, the skies gray and threatening; when our lives have no music in them, and our hearts are lonely, and our souls have lost their courage. Flood the path with light, run our eyes to where the skies are full of promise; tune our hearts to brave music; give us the sense of comradeship with heroes and saints of every age; and so quicken our spirits that we may be able to encourage the souls of all who journey with us on the road of life, to Your honor and glory.

St. Augustine

The balance of affirmation and discipline, freedom and restraint, encouragement and warning is different for each child and season and generation, yet the absolutes of God's Word are necessary and trustworthy at all times.

Gloria Gaither

Encouragement starts at home, but it should never end there.

Marie T. Freeman

Verse 24

Be energetic in your life of salvation, reverent and sensitive before God. That energy is God's energy, an energy deep within you, God himself willing and working at what will give him the most pleasure.

Energy for Today

All of us have moments when we feel exhausted. All of us suffer through tough times, difficult days, and perplexing periods of our lives. Thankfully, God promises to give us comfort and strength if we turn to Him.

If you're a person with too many demands and too few hours in which to meet them, it's probably time to examine your priorities while you pare down your daily to-do list. While you're at it, take time to focus upon God and His love for you. Then, ask Him for the wisdom to prioritize your life and the strength to fulfill your responsibilities. God will give you the energy to do the most important things on today's to-do list if you ask Him. So ask Him . . . today.

More Great Ideas About Energy

God does not dispense strength and encouragement like a druggist fills your prescription. The Lord doesn't promise to give us something to take so we can handle our weary moments. He promises us Himself. That is all. And that is enough.

Charles Swindoll

Worry does not empty tomorrow of its sorrow; it empties today of its strength.

Corrie ten Boom

One reason so much American Christianity is a mile wide and an inch deep is that Christians are simply tired. Sometimes you need to kick back and rest for Jesus' sake.

Dennis Swanberg

Sometimes I think spiritual and physical strength is like manna: you get just what you need for the day, no more.

Suzanne Dale Ezell

When we reach the end of our strength, wisdom, and personal resources, we enter into the beginning of his glorious provisions.

Patsy Clairmont

Whatever you do, do it enthusiastically, as something done for the Lord and not for men.

Colossians 3:23 HCSB

Enthusiasm Now

D o you see each day as a glorious opportunity to serve God and to do His will? Are you enthused about life, or do you struggle through each day giving scarcely a thought to God's blessings? Are you constantly praising God for His gifts, and are you sharing His Good News with the world? And are you excited about the possibilities for service that God has placed before you, whether at home, at work, at church, or at school? You should be.

You are the recipient of Christ's sacrificial love. Accept it enthusiastically and share it fervently. Jesus deserves your enthusiasm; the world deserves it; and you deserve the experience of sharing it.

More Great Ideas About Enthusiasm

Don't take hold of a thing unless you want that thing to take hold of you.

E. Stanley Jones

Enthusiasm, like the flu, is contagious—we get it from one another.

Barbara Johnson

Wherever you are, be all there. Live to the hilt every situation you believe to be the will of God.

Jim Elliot

One of the great needs in the church today is for every Christian to become enthusiastic about his faith in Jesus Christ.

Billy Graham

We act as though comfort and luxury were the chief requirements of life, when all we need to make us really happy is something to be enthusiastic about.

Charles Kingsley

Catch on fire with enthusiasm and people will come for miles to watch you burn.

John Wesley

Therefore, get your minds ready for action, being self-disciplined, and set your hope completely on the grace to be brought to you at the revelation of Jesus Christ.

1 Peter 1:13 HCSB

Beyond Excuses

Excuses and character-building don't mix. If you want to build character—and if you want to keep building it—you'll need to avoid the unseemly habit of excuse-making. No exceptions.

We live in a world where excuses are everywhere. And it's precisely because excuses are so numerous that they are also so ineffective. When we hear the words, "I'm sorry but . . . ," most of us know exactly what is to follow: The Big Excuse. The dog ate the homework. Traffic was terrible. It's the company's fault. The boss is to blame. The equipment is broken. We're out of that. And so forth, and so on.

Because we humans are such creative excuse-makers, all of the really good excuses have already been taken. In fact, the high-quality excuses have been used, re-used, over-used, and ab-used. That's why excuses don't work—we've heard them all before.

So, if you're wasting your time trying to portray yourself as a victim (and weakening your character in the process), or if you're trying to concoct a new and improved excuse, don't bother. Excuses don't work, and while you're inventing them, neither do you.

More Great Ideas About Excuses

Replace your excuses with fresh determination.

Charles Swindoll

We need to stop focusing on our lacks and stop giving out excuses and start looking at and listening to Jesus.

Anne Graham Lotz

Rationalization: It's what we do when we substitute false explanations for true reasons, when we cloud our actual motives with a smoke screen of nice-sounding excuses.

Charles Swindoll

An excuse is only the skin of a reason stuffed with a lie.

Vance Havner

Making up a string of excuses is usually harder than doing the work.

Marie T. Freeman

Let us lay aside every weight and the sin that so easily ensnares us, and run with endurance the race that lies before us, keeping our eyes on Jesus, the source and perfecter of our faith.

Hebrews 12:1-2 HCSB

What's Your Focus?

What is your focus today? Are you willing to focus your thoughts and energies on God's blessings and upon His will for your life? Or will you turn your thoughts to other things? Before you answer that question, consider this: God created you in His own image, and He wants you to experience joy and abundance. But, God will not force His joy upon you; you must claim it for yourself.

This day—and every day hereafter—is a chance to celebrate the life that God has given you. It's also a chance to give thanks to the One who has offered you more blessings than you can possibly count.

Today, why not focus your thoughts on the joy that is rightfully yours in Christ? Why not take time to celebrate God's glorious creation? Why not trust your hopes instead of your fears? When you do, you will think optimistically about yourself and your world . . . and you can then share your optimism with others.

More Great Ideas About Focus

Measure the size of the obstacles against the size of God.

Beth Moore

We need to stop focusing on our lacks and stop giving out excuses and start looking at and listening to Jesus.

Anne Graham Lotz

What is your focus today? Joy comes when it is Jesus first, others second...then you.

Kay Arthur

Don't let worry rob you of the joy that is rightfully yours. God is in heaven, and He knows your every need. Focus on God and His provisions, and watch gratefully as the worries of today begin to fade away.

Marie T. Freeman

Paul did one thing. Most of us dabble in forty things. Are you a doer or a dabbler?

Vance Havner

When Jesus is in our midst, He brings His limitless power along as well. But, Jesus must be in the middle, all eyes and hearts focused on Him.

Shirley Dobson

The greatest among you must be a servant. But those who exalt themselves will be humbled, and those who humble themselves will be exalted.

Matthew 23:11-12 NKJV

Staying Humble

As fallible human beings, we have so much to be humble about. Why, then, is humility such a difficult trait for us to master? Precisely because we are fallible human beings. Yet if we are to grow and mature as Christians, we must strive to give credit where credit is due, starting, of course, with God and His only begotten Son.

As Christians, we have been refashioned and saved by Jesus Christ, and that salvation came not because of our own good works but because of God's grace. Thus, we are not "self-made"; we are "God-made," and we are "Christ-saved." How, then, can we be boastful? The answer, of course, is that, if we are honest with ourselves and with our God, we simply can't be boastful... we must, instead, be eternally grateful and exceedingly humble. Humility, however, is not easy for most of us. All too often, we are tempted to stick out our chests and say, "Look at me; look what I did!" But, in the quiet moments when we search the depths of our own hearts, we know better. Whatever "it" is, God did that. And He deserves the credit.

Jesus had a humble heart.
If He abides in us,
pride will never
dominate our lives.

—

Billy Graham

More Great Ideas About Humility

I can usually sense that a leading is from the Holy Spirit when it calls me to humble myself, to serve somebody, to encourage somebody, or to give something away. Very rarely will the evil one lead us to do those kind of things.

Bill Hybels

If you know who you are in Christ, your personal ego is not an issue.

Beth Moore

That's what I love about serving God. In His eyes, there are no little people . . . because there are no big people. We are all on the same playing field. We all start at square one. No one has it better than the other, or possesses unfair advantage.

Joni Eareckson Tada

Because Christ Jesus came to the world clothed in humility, he will always be found among those who are clothed with humility. He will be found among the humble people.

A. W. Tozer

Faith itself cannot be strong where humility is weak.

C. H. Spurgeon

These things have I spoken unto you, that my joy might remain in you, and that your joy might be full.

John 15:11 KJV

Making His Joy Your Joy

Christ made it clear: He intends that His joy should become our joy. Yet sometimes, amid the inevitable hustle and bustle of life here on earth, we can forfeit—albeit temporarily—the joy of Christ as we wrestle with the challenges of daily living.

Jonathan Edwards, the 18th-century American clergyman, observed, "Christ is not only a remedy for your weariness and trouble, but he will give you an abundance of the contrary: joy and delight. They who come to Christ do not only come to a resting-place after they have been wandering in a wilderness, but they come to a banqueting-house where they may rest, and where they may feast. They may cease from their former troubles and toils, and they may enter upon a course of delights and spiritual joys."

If, today, your heart is heavy, open the door of your soul to Christ. He will give you peace and joy. And, if you already have the joy of Christ in your heart, share it freely, just as Christ freely shared His joy with you.

More Great Ideas About Joy

Joy is the direct result of having God's perspective on our daily lives and the effect of loving our Lord enough to obey His commands and trust His promises.

Bill Bright

If you can forgive the person you were, accept the person you are, and believe in the person you will become, you are headed for joy. So celebrate your life.

Barbara Johnson

The Christian lifestyle is not one of legalistic do's and don'ts, but one that is positive, attractive, and joyful.

Vonette Bright

Lord, I thank you for the promise of heaven and the unexpected moments when you touch my heartstrings with that longing for my eternal home.

Joni Eareckson Tada

A life of intimacy with God is characterized by joy.

Oswald Chambers

Our sense of joy, satisfaction, and fulfillment in life increases, no matter what the circumstances, if we are in the center of God's will.

Billy Graham

God knows everything. He can manage everything, and He loves us. Surely this is enough for a fullness of joy that is beyond words.

Hannah Whitall Smith

God gives to us a heavenly gift called joy, radically different in quality from any natural joy.

Elisabeth Elliot

Joy is the heart's harmonious response to the Lord's song of love.

A. W. Tozer

Rejoice, the Lord is King; Your Lord and King adore! Rejoice, give thanks and sing and triumph evermore.

Charles Wesley

Rejoice in the Lord always. Again I will say, rejoice!

Philippians 4:4 NKJV

Rejoice!

Are you living a life of agitation, consternation, or celebration? If you're a believer, it should most certainly be the latter. With Christ as your Savior, every day should be a time of celebration.

Oswald Chambers correctly observed, "Joy is the great note all throughout the Bible." C. S. Lewis echoed that thought when he wrote, "Joy is the serious business of heaven." But, even the most dedicated Christians can, on occasion, forget to celebrate each day for what it is: a priceless gift from God.

Today, celebrate the life that God has given you. Today, put a smile on your face, kind words on your lips, and a song in your heart. Be generous with your praise and free with your encouragement. And then, when you have celebrated life to the fullest, invite your friends to do likewise. After all, this is God's day, and He has given us clear instructions for its use. We are commanded to rejoice and be glad. So, with no further ado, let the celebration begin.

More Great Ideas About Celebration

According to Jesus, it is God's will that His children be filled with the joy of life.

Catherine Marshall

If our hearts have been attuned to God through an abiding faith in Christ, the result will be joyous optimism and good cheer.

Billy Graham

He is ever faithful and gives us the song in the night to soothe our spirits and fresh joy each morning to lift our souls. What a marvelous Lord!

Bill Bright

Christ is the secret, the source, the substance, the center, and the circumference of all true and lasting gladness.

Mrs. Charles E. Cowman

The highest and most desirable state of the soul is to praise God in celebration for being alive.

Luci Swindol

When the dream of our heart is one that God has planted there, a strange happiness flows into us. At that moment, all of the spiritual resources of the universe are released to help us. Our praying is then at one with the will of God and becomes a channel for the Creator's purposes for us and our world.

Catherine Marshall

Joy is a by-product not of happy circumstances, education or talent, but of a healthy relationship with God and a determination to love Him no matter what.

Barbara Johnson

When we get rid of inner conflicts and wrong attitudes toward life, we will almost automatically burst into joy.

E. Stanley Jones

Some of us seem so anxious about avoiding hell that we forget to celebrate our journey toward heaven.

Philip Yancey

True happiness and contentment cannot come from the things of this world. The blessedness of true joy is a free gift that comes only from our Lord and Savior, Jesus Christ.

Dennis Swanberg

The fear of the Lord is the beginning of wisdom, and the knowledge of the Holy One is understanding.

Proverbs 9:10 HCSB

The Right Kind of Fear

D o you have a healthy, fearful respect for God's power? If so, you are both wise and obedient. And, because you are a thoughtful believer, you also understand that genuine wisdom begins with a profound appreciation for God's limitless power.

God praises humility and punishes pride. That's why God's greatest servants will always be those humble men and women who care less for their own glory and more for God's glory. In God's kingdom, the only way to achieve greatness is to shun it. And the only way to be wise is to understand these facts: God is great; He is all-knowing; and He is all-powerful. We must respect Him, and we must humbly obey His commandments, or we must accept the consequences of our misplaced pride.

More Great Ideas About Fearing God

The remarkable thing about fearing God is that when you fear God, you fear nothing else, whereas if you do not fear God, you fear everything else.

Oswald Chambers

If we do not tremble before God, the world's system seems wonderful to us and pleasantly consumes us.

James Montgomery Boice

A healthy fear of God will do much to deter us from sin.

Charles Swindoll

It is not possible that mortal men should be thoroughly conscious of the divine presence without being filled with awe.

C. H. Spurgeon

When true believers are awed by the greatness of God and by the privilege of becoming His children, then they become sincerely motivated, effective evangelists.

Bill Hybels

I have come as a light into the world, that whoever believes in Me should not abide in darkness.

John 12:46 NKJV

Jesus Is the Light

The words of John 12:46 teach us that Jesus is the light of the world. And, John 14:6-7 instructs us that Jesus is, "the way, the truth, and the life." Without Christ, we are as far removed from salvation as the east is removed from the west. And without Christ, we can never know the ultimate truth: God's truth.

Truth is God's way: He commands His believers to live in truth, and He rewards those who do so. Jesus is the personification of God's liberating truth, a truth that offers salvation to mankind.

Do you seek to walk with God? Do you seek to feel His presence and His peace? Then you must walk in truth; you must walk in the light; you must walk with the Savior. There is simply no other way.

More Great Ideas About Jesus

When you can't see him, trust him. Jesus is closer than you ever dreamed.

Max Lucado

I am truly happy with Jesus Christ. I couldn't live without Him. When my life gets beyond the ability to cope, He takes over.

Ruth Bell Graham

In your greatest weakness, turn to your greatest strength, Jesus, and hear Him say, "My grace is sufficient for you, for My strength is made perfect in weakness" (2 Corinthians 12:9, NKJV).

Lisa Whelchel

The key to my understanding of the Bible is a personal relationship to Jesus Christ.

Oswald Chambers

Jesus—personally, socially, politically, the supreme center of human interest today.

R. G. Lee

There was One, who for "us sinners and our salvation," left the glories of heaven and sojourned upon this earth in weariness and woe, amid those who hated his and finally took his life.

Lottie Moon

Christians see sin for what it is: willful rebellion against the rulership of God in their lives. And in turning from their sin, they have embraced God's only means of dealing with sin: Jesus.

Kay Arthur

When we are in a situation where Jesus is all we have, we soon discover he is all we really need.

Gigi Graham Tchividjian

Jesus: the proof of God's love.

Philip Yancey

Jesus Christ is the first and last, author and finisher, beginning and end, alpha and omega, and by Him all other things hold together. He must be first or nothing. God never comes next!

Vance Havner

But Jesus looked at them and said to them, "With men this is impossible, but with God all things are possible."

Matthew 19:26 NKJV

All Things Are Possible

Sometimes, because we are imperfect human beings with limited understanding and limited faith, we place limitations on God. But, God's power has no limitations. God will work miracles in our lives if we trust Him with everything we have and everything we are. When we do, we experience the miraculous results of His endless love and His awesome power.

Miracles, both great and small, are an integral part of everyday life, but usually, we are too busy or too cynical to notice God's handiwork. We don't expect to see miracles, so we simply overlook them.

Do you lack the faith that God can work miracles in your own life? If so, it's time to reconsider. If you have allowed yourself to become a "doubting Thomas," you are attempting to place limitations on a God who has none. Instead of doubting your Heavenly Father, you must trust Him. Then, you must wait and watch . . . because something miraculous is going to happen to you, and it might just happen today.

More Great Ideas About Miracles

I have been suspected of being what is called a fundamentalist. That is because I never regard any narrative as unhistorical simply on the ground that it includes the miraculous.

C. S. Lewis

When we face an impossible situation, all self-reliance and self-confidence must melt away; we must be totally dependent on Him for the resources.

Anne Graham Lotz

There is Someone who makes possible what seems completely impossible.

Catherine Marshall

I could go through this day oblivious to the miracles all around me or I could tune in and "enjoy."

Gloria Gaither

We have a God who delights in impossibilities.

Andrew Murray

Only God can move mountains, but faith and prayer can move God.

E. M. Bounds

Here lies the tremendous mystery—that God should be all-powerful, yet refuse to coerce. He summons us to cooperation. We are honored in being given the opportunity to participate in His good deeds. Remember how He asked for help in performing His miracles: Fill the water pots, stretch out your hand, distribute the loaves.

Elisabeth Elliot

Are you looking for a miracle? If you keep your eyes wide open and trust in God, you won't have to look very far.

Marie T. Freeman

The miracles in fact are a retelling in small letters of the very same story which is written across the whole world in letters too large for some of us to see.

C. S. Lewis

Never be afraid to hope—or to ask—for a miracle.

Criswell Freeman

Jesus said to him, "'You shall love the Lord your God with all your heart, with all your soul, and with all your mind.' This is the first and great commandment."

Matthew 22:37-38 NKJV

Loving God

Christ's words are unambiguous: "Love the Lord your God with all your heart and with all your soul and with all your mind." But sometimes, despite our best intentions, we fall short of God's plan for our lives when we become embittered with ourselves, with our neighbors, or most especially with our Creator.

If we are to please God, we must cleanse ourselves of the negative feelings that separate us from others and from Him. In 1 Corinthians 13, we are told that love is the foundation upon which all our relationships are to be built: our relationships with others and our relationship with our Maker.

So today and every day, fill your heart with love; never yield to bitterness; and praise the Son of God who, in His infinite wisdom, made love His greatest commandment.

More Great Ideas About Loving God

I love Him because He first loved me, and He still does love me, and He will love me forever and ever.

Bill Bright

Loving Him means the thankful acceptance of all things that His love has appointed.

Elisabeth Elliot

God is so inconceivably good. He's not looking for perfection. He already saw it in Christ. He's looking for affection.

Beth Moore

God has a genuine, passionate affection for each of us and invites us to open our hearts to that love and then return love to Him with deep sincerity.

Bill Hybels

A man's spiritual health is exactly proportional to his love for God.

C. S. Lewis

Joy is a by-product not of happy circumstances, education or talent, but of a healthy relationship with God and a determination to love Him no matter what.

Barbara Johnson

Man was created by God to know and love Him in a permanent, personal relationship.

Anne Graham Lotz

Whatever you love most, be it sports, pleasure, business or God, that is your god.

Billy Graham

In true religion, to love God and to know God are synonymous terms.

C. H. Spurgeon

When an honest soul can get still before the living Christ, we can still hear Him say simply and clearly, "Love the Lord your God with all your heart and with all your soul and with all your mind…and love one another as I have loved you."

Gloria Gaither

Do not fear, for I am with you; do not be afraid, for I am your God. I will strengthen you; I will help you; I will hold on to you with My righteous right hand.

Isaiah 41:10 HCSB

Above and Beyond Fear

We live in a fear-based world, a world where bad news travels at light speed and good news doesn't. These are troubled times, times when we have legitimate fears for the future of our nation, our world, and our families. But we also have every reason to live courageously. After all, since God has promised to love us and protect us, who—or what—should we fear?

Perhaps you, like countless others, have found your courage tested by the anxieties and fears that are an inevitable part of life. If so, let the words of Isaiah 41:10 serve as a reminder that God wants to you to think less about your challenges and more about His love. Remember that He is not just near, He is here, and He's ready to help right now. God will comfort you if you ask Him to. So why not ask? And why not now?

More Great Ideas About Fear

Courage faces fear and thereby masters it. Cowardice represses fear and is thereby mastered by it.

Martin Luther King, Jr.

Whether our fear is absolutely realistic or out of proportion in our minds, our greatest refuge is Jesus Christ.

Luci Swindoll

Only believe, don't fear. Our Master, Jesus, always watches over us, and no matter what the persecution, Jesus will surely overcome it.

Lottie Moon

Fear and doubt are conquered by a faith that rejoices. And faith can rejoice because the promises of God are as certain as God Himself.

Kay Arthur

When once we are assured that God is good, then there can be nothing left to fear.

Hannah Whitall Smith

Our future may look fearfully intimidating, yet we can look up to the Engineer of the Universe, confident that nothing escapes His attention or slips out of the control of those strong hands.

Elisabeth Elliot

Earthly fears are no fears at all. Answer the big question of eternity, and the little questions of life fall into perspective.

Max Lucado

There is not only fear, but terrible danger, for the life unguarded by God.

Oswald Chambers

Are you fearful? First, bow your head and pray for God's strength. Then, raise your head and look Old Man Trouble squarely in the eye. Chances are, Old Man Trouble will blink.

Jim Gallery

The Bible is a Christian's guidebook, and I believe the knowledge it sheds on pain and suffering is the great antidote to fear for suffering people. Knowledge can dissolve fear as light destroys darkness.

Philip Yancey

The LORD is gracious and full of compassion, slow to anger and great in mercy. The LORD is good to all, and His tender mercies are over all His works.

Psalm 145:8-9 NKJV

God's Mercy

In Psalm 145, we are taught that God is merciful. His hand offers forgiveness and salvation. God's mercy, like His love, is infinite and everlasting—it knows no boundaries.

Romans 3:23 reminds us of a universal truth: "All have sinned, and come short of the glory of God" (KJV). All of us, even the most righteous among us, are sinners. But despite our imperfections, our merciful Father in heaven offers us salvation through the person of His Son.

As Christians, we have been blessed by a merciful, loving God. Now, it's our turn to share His love and His mercy with a world that needs both. May we accept His gifts and share them with our friends, with our families, and with all the people He chooses to place along our paths.

More Great Ideas About God's Mercy

Mercy is an attribute of God, an infinite and inexhaustible energy within the divine nature which disposes God to be actively compassionate.

A. W. Tozer

How happy we are when we realize that He is responsible, that He goes before, that goodness and mercy shall follow us!

Mrs. Charles E. Cowman

Is your child learning of the love of God through your love, tenderness, and mercy?

James Dobson

When terrible things happen, there are two choices, and only two: We can trust God, or we can defy Him. We believe that God is God, He's still got the whole world in His hands and knows exactly what He's doing, or we must believe that He is not God and that we are at the awful mercy of mere chance.

Elisabeth Elliot

Looking back over my life, all I can see is mercy and grace written in large letters everywhere. May God help me have the same kind of heart toward those who wound or offend me.

Jim Cymbala

Trust the past to the mercy of God, the present to his love, and the future to his Providence.

St. Augustine

Angels descending, bring from above, Echoes of mercy, whispers of love.

Fanny Crosby

The Creator has given to us the awesome responsibility of representing him to our children. Our heavenly Father is a God of unlimited love, and our children must become acquainted with his mercy and tenderness through our own love toward them.

James Dobson

Storm the throne of grace and persevere therein, and mercy will come down.

John Wesley

Verse 37

Blessed is the man who walks not in the counsel of the ungodly, nor stands in the path of sinners, nor sits in the seat of the scornful; but his delight is in the law of the Lord, and in His law he meditates day and night.

Psalm 1:1-2 NKJV

Walking with the Righteous

Peer pressure can be a good thing or a bad thing, depending upon your peers. If your peers encourage you to make integrity a habit—and if they encourage you to follow God's will and to obey His commandments—then you'll experience positive peer pressure, and that's good. But, if you are involved with people who encourage you to do foolish things, you're facing a different kind of peer pressure . . . and you'd better beware. When you feel pressured to do things or to say things that lead you away from God, you're aiming straight for trouble.

Are you satisfied to follow that crowd? If so, you may pay a heavy price unless you've picked the right crowd. And while you're deciding whom to follow, be sure you're determined to follow the One from Galilee, too.

Jesus will guide your steps and bless your undertakings if you let Him. Your challenge, of course, is to let Him.

To sum it up, here's your choice: you can choose to please God first (and by doing so, strengthen your character), or you can fall prey to peer pressure. The choice is yours—and so are the consequences.

You will get untold flak for prioritizing God's revealed and present will for your life over man's . . . but, boy, is it worth it.

—

Beth Moore

More Great Ideas About Peer Pressure

Do you want to be wise? Choose wise friends.

Charles Swindoll

It is comfortable to know that we are responsible to God and not to man. It is a small matter to be judged of man's judgement.

Lottie Moon

We, as God's people, are not only to stay far away from sin and sinners who would entice us, but we are to be so like our God that we mourn over sin.

Kay Arthur

Comparison is the root of all feelings of inferiority.

James Dobson

You should forget about trying to be popular with everybody and start trying to be popular with God Almighty.

Sam Jones

*Even though I walk through the valley of the shadow of death,
I will fear no evil, for you are with me; your rod and your
staff, they comfort me.*

Psalm 23:4 NIV

Trust the Shepherd

In the 23rd Psalm, David teaches us that God is like a watchful shepherd caring for His flock. No wonder these verses have provided comfort and hope for generations of believers.

You are precious in the eyes of God. You are His priceless creation, made in His image, and protected by Him. God watches over every step you make and every breath you take, so you need never be afraid. But sometimes, fear has a way of slipping into the minds and hearts of even the most devout believers—and you are no exception.

You know from firsthand experience that life is not always easy. But as a recipient of God's grace, you also know that you are protected by a loving Heavenly Father.

On occasion, you will confront circumstances that trouble you to the very core of your soul. When you are afraid, trust in God. When you are worried, turn your concerns over to Him. When you are anxious, be still and listen for the quiet assurance of God's promises. And then, place your life in His hands. He is your Shepherd today and throughout eternity. Trust the Shepherd.

When God allows extraordinary
trials for His people,
He prepares extraordinary
comforts for them.

—

Corrie ten Boom

More Great Ideas About God's Comfort

When I am criticized, injured, or afraid, there is a Father who is ready to comfort me.

Max Lucado

Put your hand into the hand of God. He gives the calmness and serenity of heart and soul.

Mrs. Charles E. Cowman

We all go through pain and sorrow, but the presence of God, like a warm, comforting blanket, can shield us and protect us, and allow the deep inner joy to surface, even in the most devastating circumstances.

Barbara Johnson

The God of the galaxies is the God who knows when your heart is broken—and He can heal it!

Warren Wiersbe

You don't have to be alone in your hurt! Comfort is yours. Joy is an option. And it's all been made possible by your Savior. He went without comfort so you might have it. He postponed joy so you might share in it. He willingly chose isolation so you might never be alone in your hurt and sorrow.

Joni Eareckson Tada

God is our refuge and strength, a very present help in trouble.

Psalm 46:1 NKJV

God Is Our Refuge

The words of Psalm 46:1 promise that God is our refuge, a refuge that we all need. From time to time, all of us face adversity, discouragement, or disappointment. And throughout life, we all must endure life-changing personal losses that leave us breathless. When we do, God stands ready to protect us. Psalm 147 assures us that, "He heals the brokenhearted, and binds their wounds" (v. 3, NIV).

Are you anxious? Take those anxieties to God. Are you troubled? Take your troubles to Him. Does the world seem to be trembling beneath your feet? Seek protection from the One who cannot be moved.

The same God who created the universe stands ready and willing to comfort you and to restore your strength. During life's most difficult days, your Heavenly Father remains steadfast. And, in His own time and according to His master plan, He will heal you if you invite Him into your heart.

More Great Ideas About Tough Times

The sermon of your life in tough times ministers to people more powerfully than the most eloquent speaker.

Bill Bright

Faith is a strong power, mastering any difficulty in the strength of the Lord who made heaven and earth.

Corrie ten Boom

If all struggles and sufferings were eliminated, the spirit would no more reach maturity than would the child.

Elisabeth Elliot

God will never let you sink under your circumstances. He always provides a safety net and His love always encircles.

Barbara Johnson

Sometimes we get tired of the burdens of life, but we know that Jesus Christ will meet us at the end of life's journey. And, that makes all the difference.

Billy Graham

Measure the size of the obstacles against the size of God.

Beth Moore

Even in the winter, even in the midst of the storm, the sun is still there. Somewhere, up above the clouds, it still shines and warms and pulls at the life buried deep inside the brown branches and frozen earth. The sun is there! Spring will come.

Gloria Gaither

God allows us to experience the low points of life in order to teach us lessons that we could learn in no other way.

C. S. Lewis

Our loving God uses difficulty in our lives to burn away the sin of self and build faith and spiritual power.

Bill Bright

Adversity is always unexpected and unwelcomed. It is an intruder and a thief, and yet in the hands of God, adversity becomes the means through which His supernatural power is demonstrated.

Charles Swindoll

Unless the Lord builds a house, its builders labor over it in vain; unless the Lord watches over a city, the watchman stays alert in vain.

Psalm 127:1 HCSB

He Watches Over Us

Have you ever faced challenges that seemed too big to handle? Have you ever faced big problems that, despite your best efforts, simply could not be solved? If so, you know how uncomfortable it is to feel helpless in the face of difficult circumstances. Thankfully, even when there's nowhere else to turn, you can turn your thoughts and prayers to God, and He will respond.

God's hand uplifts those who turn their hearts and prayers to Him. Count yourself among that number. When you do, you can live courageously and joyfully, knowing that "this too will pass"—but that God's love for you will not. And you can draw strength from the knowledge that you are a marvelous creation, loved, protected, and uplifted by the ever-present hand of God.

More Great Ideas About
God's Protection

When you fall and skin your knees and skin your heart,
He'll pick you up.

Charles Stanley

In all the old castles of England, there was a place called
the keep. It was always the strongest and best protected
place in the castle, and in it were hidden all who were
weak and helpless and unable to defend themselves in
times of danger. Shall we be afraid to hide ourselves in
the keeping power of our Divine Keeper, who neither
slumbers nor sleeps, and who has promised to preserve
our going out and our coming in, from this time forth
and even forever more?

Hannah Whitall Smith

Trials are not enemies of faith but opportunities to reveal
God's faithfulness.

Barbara Johnson

There is no safer place to live than the center of His will.

Calvin Miller

Gather the riches of God's promises which can strengthen you in the time when there will be no freedom.

Corrie ten Boom

Our future may look fearfully intimidating, yet we can look up to the Engineer of the Universe, confident that nothing escapes His attention or slips out of the control of those strong hands.

Elisabeth Elliot

Through all of the crises of life—and we all are going to experience them—we have this magnificent Anchor.

Franklin Graham

My case is urgent, and I do not see how I am to be delivered; but this is no business of mine. He who makes the promise will find ways and means of keeping it. It is mine to obey His command; it is not mine to direct His counsels. I am His servant, not His solicitor. I call upon Him, and He will deliver.

C. H. Spurgeon

God delights in spreading His protective wings and enfolding His frightened, weary, beaten-down, worn-out children.

Bill Hybels

The sensible see danger and take cover; the foolish keep going and are punished.

Proverbs 27:12 HCSB

Plan Ahead . . . and Work Hard

Are you willing to plan for the future—and are you willing to work diligently to accomplish the plans that you've made? The Book of Proverbs teaches that the plans of hardworking people (like you) are rewarded.

If you desire to reap a bountiful harvest from life, you must plan for the future while entrusting the final outcome to God. Then, you must do your part to make the future better (by working dutifully), while acknowledging the sovereignty of God's hands over all affairs, including your own.

Are you in a hurry for success to arrive at your doorstep? Don't be. Instead, work carefully, plan thoughtfully, and wait patiently. Remember that you're not the only one working on your behalf: God, too, is at work. And with Him as your partner, your ultimate success is guaranteed.

More Great Ideas About Planning

You can't start building a better tomorrow if you wait till tomorrow to start building.

Marie T. Freeman

The only way you can experience abundant life is to surrender your plans to Him.

Charles Stanley

Allow your dreams a place in your prayers and plans. God-given dreams can help you move into the future He is preparing for you.

Barbara Johnson

Plan ahead—it wasn't raining when Noah built the ark.

Anonymous

We should not be upset when unexpected and upsetting things happen. God, in his wisdom, means to make something of us which we have not yet attained, and He is dealing with us accordingly.

J. I. Packer

God has a plan for your life . . . do you?

Criswell Freeman

Our problem is that we become too easily enamored with our own plans.

Henry Blackaby

Our heavenly Father never takes anything from his children unless he means to give them something better.

George Mueller

When you become consumed by God's call on your life, everything will take on new meaning and significance. You will begin to see every facet of your life—including your pain—as a means through which God can work to bring others to Himself.

Charles Swindoll

We are not necessarily doubting that God will do the best for us; we are wondering how painful the best will turn out to be.

C. S. Lewis

If you have faith as a mustard seed, you will say to this mountain, "Move from here to there," and it will move; and nothing will be impossible for you.

Matthew 17:20 NKJV

Mountain-Moving Faith

B ecause we live in a demanding world, all of us have mountains to climb and mountains to move. Moving those mountains requires faith.

Are you a mountain mover whose faith is evident for all to see? Or, are you a spiritual shrinking violet? God needs more men and women who are willing to move mountains for His glory and for His kingdom.

Jesus taught His disciples that if they had faith, they could move mountains. You can too. When you place your faith, your trust, indeed your life in the hands of Christ Jesus, you'll be amazed at the marvelous things He can do. So strengthen your faith through praise, through worship, through Bible study, and through prayer. And trust God's plans. With Him, all things are possible, and He stands ready to open a world of possibilities to you . . . if you have faith.

Concentration camp survivor Corrie ten Boom re-lied on faith during her long months of imprisonment and torture. Later, despite the fact that four of her family members had died in Nazi death camps, Corrie's faith was unshaken. She wrote, "There is no pit so deep that God's love is not deeper still." Christians take note: Genuine faith in God means faith in all circumstances, happy or sad, joyful or tragic.

If your faith is being tested to the point of breaking, remember that your Savior is near. If you reach out to Him in faith, He will give you peace and strength. Reach out today. If you touch even the smallest fragment of the Master's garment, He will make you whole. And then, with no further ado, let the mountain moving begin.

I am truly grateful that faith enables me to move past the question of "Why?"

—

Zig Ziglar

More Great Ideas About Faith

There are a lot of things in life that are difficult to understand. Faith allows the soul to go beyond what the eyes can see.

John Maxwell

Faith is seeing light with the eyes of your heart, when the eyes of your body see only darkness.

Barbara Johnson

Just as our faith strengthens our prayer life, so do our prayers deepen our faith. Let us pray often, starting today, for a deeper, more powerful faith.

Shirley Dobson

Faith does not concern itself with the entire journey. One step is enough.

Mrs. Charles E. Cowman

When you enroll in the "school of faith," you never know what may happen next. The life of faith presents challenges that keep you going—and keep you growing!

Warren Wiersbe

So teach us to number our days, that we may gain a heart of wisdom.

Psalm 90:12 NKJV

The Gift of Life

L ife is a glorious gift from God. Treat it that way.
This day, like every other, is filled to the brim with opportunities, challenges, and choices. But, no choice that you make is more important than the choice you make concerning God. Today, you will either place Him at the center of your life—or not—and the consequences of that choice have implications that are both temporal and eternal.

Sometimes, we don't intentionally neglect God; we simply allow ourselves to become overwhelmed with the demands of everyday life. And then, without our even realizing it, we gradually drift away from the One we need most. Thankfully, God never drifts away from us. He remains always present, always steadfast, always loving.

As you begin this day, place God and His Son where they belong: in your head, in your prayers, on your lips, and in your heart. And then, with God as your guide and companion, let the journey begin.

More Great Ideas About Life

You have a glorious future in Christ! Live every moment in His power and love.

Vonette Bright

Your life is not a boring stretch of highway. It's a straight line to heaven. And just look at the fields ripening along the way. Look at the tenacity and endurance. Look at the grains of righteousness. You'll have quite a crop at harvest…so don't give up!

Joni Eareckson Tada

The value of a life can only be estimated by its relationship to God.

Oswald Chambers

A life lived without reflection can be very superficial and empty.

Elisabeth Elliot

The whole point of this life is the healing of the heart's eye through which God is seen.

St. Augustine

Jesus wants Life for us, Life with a capital L.

John Eldredge

As I contemplate all the sacrifices required in order to live a life that is totally focused on Jesus Christ and His eternal kingdom, the joy seeps out of my heart onto my face in a smile of deep satisfaction.

Anne Graham Lotz

The world has never been stable. Jesus Himself was born into the cruelest and most unstable of worlds. No, we have babies and keep trusting and living because the Resurrection is true! The Resurrection was not just a one-time event in history; it is a principle built into the very fabric of our beings, a fact reverberating from every cell of creation: Life wins! Life wins!

Gloria Gaither

Our Lord is the Bread of Life. His proportions are perfect. There never was too much or too little of anything about Him. Feed on Him for a well-balanced ration. All the vitamins and calories are there.

Vance Havner

Go, therefore, and make disciples of all nations, baptizing them in the name of the Father and of the Son and of the Holy Spirit, teaching them to observe everything I have commanded you. And remember, I am with you always, to the end of the age.

Matthew 28:19-20 HCSB

The Great Commission

Are you a bashful Christian, one who is afraid to speak up for your Savior? Do you leave it up to others to share their testimonies while you stand on the sidelines, reluctant to share yours? Too many of us are slow to obey the last commandment of the risen Christ; we don't do our best to "make disciples of all the nations."

Christ's Great Commission applies to Christians of every generation, including our own. As believers, we are commanded to share the Good News with our families, with our neighbors, and with the world. Jesus invited His disciples to become fishers of men. We, too, must accept the Savior's invitation, and we must do so today. Tomorrow may indeed be too late.

More Great Ideas About the Great Commission

You cannot keep silent once you have experienced salvation of Jesus Christ.

Warren Wiersbe

Our commission is quite specific. We are told to be His witness to all nations. For us, as His disciples, to refuse any part of this commission frustrates the love of Jesus Christ, the Son of God.

Catherine Marshall

There are many timid souls whom we jostle morning and evening as we pass them by; but if only the kind word were spoken they might become fully persuaded.

Fanny Crosby

If we are ever going to be or do anything for our Lord, now is the time.

Vance Havner

How many people have you made homesick for God?

Oswald Chambers

Your light is the truth of the Gospel message itself as well as your witness as to Who Jesus is and what He has done for you. Don't hide it.

Anne Graham Lotz

There is nothing anybody else can do that can stop God from using us. We can turn everything into a testimony.

Corrie ten Boom

Choose Jesus Christ! Deny yourself, take up the Cross, and follow Him—for the world must be shown. The world must see, in us, a discernible, visible, startling difference.

Elisabeth Elliot

There is nothing more appealing or convincing to a watching world than to hear the testimony of someone who has just been with Jesus.

Henry Blackaby

To stand in an uncaring world and say, "See, here is the Christ" is a daring act of courage.

Calvin Miller

I have set before you life and death, blessing and curse.
Choose life so that you and your descendants may live, love
the Lord your God, obey Him, and remain faithful to Him.
For He is your life, and He will prolong your life in the land
the Lord swore to give to your fathers Abraham, Isaac, and
Jacob.

Deuteronomy 30:19-20 HCSB

Making Good Choices

L ife is a series of choices. From the instant we wake in the morning until the moment we nod off to sleep at night, we make countless decisions: decisions about the things we do, decisions about the words we speak, and decisions about the thoughts we choose to think. Simply put, the quality of those decisions determines the quality of our lives.

As believers who have been saved by a loving and merciful God, we have every reason to make wise choices. Yet sometimes, amid the inevitable hustle and bustle of life here on earth, we allow ourselves to behave in ways that we know are displeasing to God. When we do, we forfeit—albeit temporarily—the joy and the peace that we might otherwise experience through Him.

As you consider the next step in your life's journey, take time to consider how many things in this life you can control: your thoughts, your words, your priorities, and your actions, for starters. And then, if you sincerely want to discover God's purpose for your life, make choices that are pleasing to Him. He deserves no less . . . and neither do you.

Every time you make a choice,
you are turning the central part of you,
the part that chooses,
into something a little different
from what it was before.

C. S. *Lewis*

More Great Ideas About Choices

Every day of our lives we make choices about how we're going to live that day.

Luci Swindoll

There may be no trumpet sound or loud applause when we make a right decision, just a calm sense of resolution and peace.

Gloria Gaither

Every day, I find countless opportunities to decide whether I will obey God and demonstrate my love for Him or try to please myself or the world system. God is waiting for my choices.

Bill Bright

Life is pretty much like a cafeteria line—it offers us many choices, both good and bad. The Christian must have a spiritual radar that detects the difference not only between bad and good but also among good, better, and best.

Dennis Swanberg

Be an example to the believers in word, in conduct, in love, in spirit, in faith, in purity.

1 Timothy 4:12 NKJV

Being the Right Kind of Example

Whether we like it or not, all of us are role models. Our friends and family members watch our actions and, as followers of Christ, we are obliged to act accordingly.

What kind of example are you? Are you the kind of person whose life serves as a genuine example of righteousness? Are you a person whose behavior serves as a positive role model for others? Are you the kind of person whose actions, day in and day out, are based upon kindness, faithfulness, and a love for the Lord? If so, you are not only blessed by God, but you are also a powerful force for good in a world that desperately needs positive influences such as yours.

We live in a dangerous, temptation-filled world. That's why you encounter so many opportunities to stray from God's commandments. Resist those temptations! When you do, you'll earn God's blessings and you'll serve as a positive role model for your family and friends.

Corrie ten Boom advised, "Don't worry about what you do not understand. Worry about what you do understand in the Bible but do not live by." And that's sound advice because our families and friends are watching . . . and so, for that matter, is God.

You can never separate a leader's actions from his character.

—

John Maxwell

More Great Ideas About
Setting the Right Kind of Example

Among the most joyful people I have known have been some who seem to have had no human reason for joy. The sweet fragrance of Christ has shown through their lives.

Elisabeth Elliot

We must mirror God's love in the midst of a world full of hatred. We are the mirrors of God's love, so we may show Jesus by our lives.

Corrie ten Boom

Integrity of heart is indispensable.

John Calvin

If I take care of my character, my reputation will take care of itself.

D. L. Moody

There is no way to grow a saint overnight. Character, like the oak tree, does not spring up like a mushroom.

Vance Havner

Now godliness with contentment is great gain. For we brought nothing into this world, and it is certain we can carry nothing out. And having food and clothing, with these we shall be content.

1 Timothy 6:6-8 NKJV

Keep It Simple

You live in a world where simplicity is in short supply. Think for a moment about the complexity of your everyday life and compare it to the lives of your ancestors. Certainly, you are the beneficiary of many technological innovations, but those innovations have a price: in all likelihood, your world is highly complex. Consider the following:

1. From the moment you wake up in the morning until the time you lay your head on the pillow at night, you are the target of an endless stream of advertising information. Each message is intended to grab your attention in order to convince you to purchase things you didn't know you needed (and probably don't!).

2. Essential aspects of your life, including personal matters such as health care, are subject to an ever-increasing flood of rules and regulations.

3. Unless you take firm control of your time and your life, you may be overwhelmed by an ever-increasing tidal wave of complexity that threatens your happiness.

Your Heavenly Father understands the joy of living simply, and so should you. So do yourself a favor: keep your life as simple as possible. Simplicity is, indeed, genius. By simplifying your life, you are destined to improve it.

Efficiency is enhanced not by what we accomplish but more often by what we relinquish.

—

Charles Swindoll

More Great Ideas About Simplicity

Prescription for a happier and healthier life: resolve to slow down your pace; learn to say no gracefully; resist the temptation to chase after more pleasure, more hobbies, and more social entanglements.

James Dobson

There is absolutely no evidence that complexity and materialism lead to happiness. On the contrary, there is plenty of evidence that simplicity and spirituality lead to joy, a blessedness that is better than happiness.

Dennis Swanberg

We Christians must simplify our lives or lose untold treasures on earth and in eternity. Modern civilization is so complex as to make the devotional life all but impossible. The need for solitude and quietness was never greater than it is today.

A. W. Tozer

All that a Christian does, even in eating and sleeping, is prayer, when it is done in simplicity, according to the order of God, without either adding to or diminishing from it by His choice.

John Wesley

Draw near to God, and He will draw near to you.

James 4:8 HCSB

Draw Near to God

If God is everywhere, why does He sometimes seem so far away? The answer to that question, of course, has nothing to do with God and everything to do with us.

When we begin each day on our knees, in praise and worship to Him, God often seems very near indeed. But, if we ignore God's presence or—worse yet—rebel against it altogether, the world in which we live becomes a spiritual wasteland.

Are you tired, discouraged or fearful? Be comforted because God is with you. Are you confused? Listen to the quiet voice of your Heavenly Father. Are you bitter? Talk with God and seek His guidance. Are you celebrating a great victory? Thank God and praise Him. He is the Giver of all things good.

In whatever condition you find yourself, wherever you are, whether you are happy or sad, victorious or vanquished, troubled or triumphant, celebrate God's presence. And be comforted. God is not just near; He has promised that He is right here, right now. And that's a promise you can depend on.

More Great Ideas About God's Presence

If you want to hear God's voice clearly and you are uncertain, then remain in His presence until He changes that uncertainty. Often, much can happen during this waiting for the Lord. Sometimes, He changes pride into humility, doubt into faith and peace.

Corrie ten Boom

If your heart has grown cold, it is because you have moved away from the fire of His presence.

Beth Moore

Make the least of all that goes and the most of all that comes. Don't regret what is past. Cherish what you have. Look forward to all that is to come. And most important of all, rely moment by moment on Jesus Christ.

Gigi Graham Tchividjian

God walks with us. He scoops us up in His arms or simply sits with us in silent strength until we cannot avoid the awesome recognition that yes, even now, He is here.

Gloria Gaither

The next time you hear a baby laugh or see an ocean wave, take note. Pause and listen as his Majesty whispers ever so gently, "I'm here."

Max Lucado

Get into the habit of dealing with God about everything. Unless, in the first waking moment of the day you learn to fling the door wide back and let God in, you will work on a wrong level all day. But, swing the door wide open and pray to your Father in secret, and every public thing will be stamped with the presence of God.

Oswald Chambers

There is a basic urge: the longing for unity. You desire a reunion with God—with God your Father.

E. Stanley Jones

God does not dispense strength and encouragement like a druggist fills your prescription. The Lord doesn't promise to give us something to take so we can handle our weary moments. He promises us Himself. That is all. And that is enough.

Charles Swindoll

But the fruit of the Spirit is love, joy, peace, patience, kindness, goodness, faith, gentleness, self-control. Against such things there is no law.

Galatians 5:22-23 HCSB

The Fruit of the Spirit

In Galatians 5, we are also told that when people live by the Spirit, they will bear "fruit of the Spirit." But what, exactly, is the fruit of the Spirit? It's a way of behaving yourself, a way of treating other people, and a way of showing the world what it means to be a Christian. The Bible says, "The fruit of the Spirit is love, joy, peace, patience, kindness, goodness, faith, gentleness, self-control."

Today and every day, will you strive to be patient, joyful, loving, and kind? Will you really try to control yourself? And while you're at it, will you be peaceful, gentle, patient, and faithful? If so, you'll demonstrate to the world that the fruit of the Spirit can make a wonderful difference in the lives of good Christian people— people like you!

More Great Ideas About
the Fruit of the Spirit

Some people have received Christ but have never reached spiritual maturity. We should grow as Christians every day, and we are not completely mature until we live in the presence of Christ.

Billy Graham

Though we, as Christians, are like Christ, having the first fruits of the Spirit, we are unlike Him, having the remainders of the flesh.

Thomas Watson

The Holy Spirit cannot be located as a guest in a house. He invades everything.

Oswald Chambers

The Holy Spirit is like a living and continually flowing fountain in believers. We have the boundless privilege of tapping into that fountain every time we pray.

Shirley Dobson

The more we abide in Christ, the more fruit we bear.

Warren Wiersbe

He did it with all his heart. So he prospered.

2 Chronicles 31:21 NKJV

Putting Yourself and Your Heart Into Your Work

The old adage is both familiar and true: We must pray as if everything depended upon God, but work as if everything depended upon us. Yet sometimes, when we are weary and discouraged, we may allow our worries to sap our energy and our hope. God has other intentions. God intends that we pray for things, and He intends that we be willing to work for the things that we pray for. More importantly, God intends that our work should become His work.

Whether you're in school or in the workplace, your success will depend, in large part, upon the passion that you bring to your work. God has created a world in which diligence is rewarded and sloth is not. So whatever you choose to do, do it with commitment, with excitement, with enthusiasm, and with vigor.

God did not create you for a life of mediocrity; He created you for far greater things. Reaching for greater things usually requires work and lots of it, which is perfectly fine with God. After all, He knows that you're up to the task, and He has big plans for you.

More Great Ideas About Passion

If your heart has grown cold, it is because you have moved away from the fire of His presence.

Beth Moore

Life is too short to spend it being angry, bored, or dull.

Barbara Johnson

Success or failure can be pretty well predicted by the degree to which the heart is fully in it.

John Eldredge

Normal does not mean average. Average run-of-the-mill Christianity is our main problem. We have confused luke-warmness with the norm. The vast majority of Sunday-morning parishioners take pride in being middle-of-the-roaders. The New Testament Christian lives above the average.

Vance Havner

One of the great needs in the church today is for every Christian to become enthusiastic about his faith in Jesus Christ.

Billy Graham

We honor God by asking for great things when they are part of His promise. We dishonor Him and cheat ourselves when we ask for molehills where He has offered mountains.

Vance Havner

Wouldn't it make astounding difference, not only in the quality of the work we do, but also in the satisfaction, even our joy, if we recognized God's gracious gift in every single task?

Elisabeth Elliot

When we wholeheartedly commit ourselves to God, there is nothing mediocre or run-of-the-mill about us. To live for Christ is to be passionate about our Lord and about our lives.

Jim Gallery

Everything you love is what makes a life worth living.

John Eldredge

In fact, when we were with you, this is what we commanded you: "If anyone isn't willing to work, he should not eat."

2 Thessalonians 3:10 HCSB

We're Expected to Work

God's Word teaches us the value of hard work. In his second letter to the Thessalonians, Paul warns, "If anyone isn't willing to work, he should not eat." And the Book of Proverbs proclaims, "One who is slack in his work is brother to one who destroys" (18:9 NIV). In short, God has created a world in which diligence is rewarded but sloth is not. So, whatever it is that you choose to do, do it with commitment, excitement, and vigor.

Hard work is not simply a proven way to get ahead; it's also part of God's plan for you. God did not create you for a life of mediocrity; He created you for far greater things. Reaching for greater things usually requires work and lots of it, which is perfectly fine with God. After all, He knows that you're up to the task, and He has big plans for you if you possess a loving heart and willing hands.

More Great Ideas About Work

Ordinary work, which is what most of us do most of the time, is ordained by God every bit as much as is the extraordinary.

Elisabeth Elliot

You can't climb the ladder of life with your hands in your pockets.

Barbara Johnson

Great relief and satisfaction can come from seeking God's priorities for us in each season, discerning what is "best" in the midst of many noble opportunities, and pouring our most excellent energies into those things.

Beth Moore

If you honor God with your work, He will honor you because of your work.

Marie T. Freeman

We must trust as if it all depended on God and work as if it all depended on us.

C. H. Spurgeon

Thank God every morning when you get up that you have something which must be done, whether you like it or not. Work breeds a hundred virtues that idleness never knows.

Charles Kingsley

It may be that the day of judgment will dawn tomorrow; in that case, we shall gladly stop working for a better tomorrow. But not before.

Dietrich Bonhoeffer

The world does not consider labor a blessing, therefore it flees and hates it, but the pious who fear the Lord labor with a ready and cheerful heart, for they know God's command, and they acknowledge His calling.

Martin Luther

Few things fire up a person's commitment like dedication to excellence.

John Maxwell

In the very place where God has put us, whatever its limitations, whatever kind of work it may be, we may indeed serve the Lord Christ.

Elisabeth Elliot

Make no friendship with an angry man, and with a furious man do not go, lest you learn his ways and set a snare for your soul.

Proverbs 22:24-25 NKJV

Dealing with Difficult People

Face it: sometimes people can be difficult to deal with . . . very, very difficult. When other people are unkind to you, you may be tempted to strike back, either verbally or in some other way. Resist that temptation. Instead, remember that God corrects other people's behaviors in His own way, and He doesn't need your help (even if you're totally convinced that He does).

So when other people behave cruelly, foolishly, or impulsively—as they will from time to time—don't respond in kind. Instead, speak up for yourself as politely as you can, and walk away. Then, forgive everybody as quickly as you can and leave the rest up to God.

More Great Ideas About Difficult People

When something robs you of your peace of mind, ask yourself if it is worth the energy you are expending on it. If not, then put it out of your mind in an act of discipline. Every time the thought of "it" returns, refuse it.

Kay Arthur

You can be sure you are abiding in Christ if you are able to have a Christlike love toward the people that irritate you the most.

Vonette Bright

A pessimist is someone who believes that when her cup runneth over she'll need a mop.

Barbara Johnson

If some hypocrites do intrude among us, it should not astonish us.

C. H. Spurgeon

Sour godliness is the devil's religion.

John Wesley

Discouraged people, if they must be discouraged, ought, at least, to keep their discouragements to themselves, hidden away in the privacy of their own bosoms lest they should discourage the hearts of their brethren.

Hannah Whitall Smith

You don't have to attend every argument you're invited to!

Anonymous

Some folks cause happiness wherever they go, others whenever they go.

Barbara Johnson

A keen sense of humor helps us to overlook the unbecoming, understand the unconventional, tolerate the unpleasant, overcome the unexpected, and outlast the unbearable.

Billy Graham

We are all fallen creatures and all very hard to live with.

C. S. Lewis

Give thanks to the Lord, for He is good; His faithful love endures forever.

Psalm 106:1 HCSB

His Love Endures

God's love for you is bigger and better than you can imagine. In fact, God's love is far too big to comprehend (in this lifetime). But this much we know: God loves you so much that He sent His Son Jesus to come to this earth and to die for you. And, when you accepted Jesus into your heart, God gave you a gift that is more precious than gold: the gift of eternal life. Now, precisely because you are a wondrous creation treasured by God, a question presents itself: What will you do in response to God's love? Will you ignore it or embrace it? Will you return it or neglect it? The decision, of course, is yours and yours alone.

When you embrace God's love, you are forever changed. When you embrace God's love, you feel differently about yourself, your neighbors, and your world. When you embrace God's love, you share His message and you obey His commandments.

When you accept the Father's gift of grace, you are blessed here on earth and throughout all eternity. So do yourself a favor right now: accept God's love with open arms and welcome His Son Jesus into your heart. When you do, your life will be changed today, tomorrow, and forever.

Being loved by Him whose opinion matters most gives us the security to risk loving, too— even loving ourselves.

—

Gloria Gaither

More Great Ideas About God's Love

Even when we cannot see the why and wherefore of God's dealings, we know that there is love in and behind them, so we can rejoice always.

J. I. Packer

God proved his love on the cross. When Christ hung, and bled, and died, it was God saying to the world—I love you.

Billy Graham

I think God knew that the message we sometimes need to hear today is not what a great and mighty God we serve, but rather what a tender, loving Father we have, even when He says no.

Lisa Whelchel

Every tiny bit of my life that has value I owe to the redemption of Jesus Christ. Am I doing anything to enable Him to bring His redemption into evident reality in the lives of others?

Oswald Chambers

155

No temptation has overtaken you except such as is common to man; but God is faithful, who will not allow you to be tempted beyond what you are able, but with the temptation will also make the way of escape, that you may be able to bear it.

1 Corinthians 10:13 NKJV

Resisting Temptation

It's inevitable: today you will be tempted by somebody or something—in fact, you will probably be tempted many times. Why? Because you live in a world that is filled to the brim with temptations! Some of these temptations are small; eating a second scoop of ice cream, for example, is enticing but not very dangerous. Other temptations, however, are not nearly so harmless.

The devil is working 24/7, and he's causing pain and heartache in more ways than ever before. We, as believers, must remain watchful and strong. And the good news is this: When it comes to fighting Satan, we are never alone. God is always with us, and He gives us the power to resist temptation whenever we ask Him to give us strength.

In a letter to believers, Peter offered a stern warning: "Your adversary, the devil, prowls around like a roaring lion, seeking someone to devour" (1 Peter 5:8 NASB). As Christians, we must take that warning seriously, and we must behave accordingly.

Since you are tempted
without ceasing,
pray without ceasing.

—

C. H. Spurgeon

More Great Ideas About Temptation

There is sharp necessity for giving Christ absolute obedience. The devil bids for our complete self-will. To whatever extent we give this self-will the right to be master over our lives, we are, to an extent, giving Satan a toehold.

Catherine Marshall

Instant intimacy is one of the leading warning signals of a seduction.

Beth Moore

Flee temptation without leaving a forwarding address.

Barbara Johnson

It is easier to stay out of temptation than to get out of it.

Rick Warren

A man who gives in to temptation after five minutes simply does not know what it would have been like an hour later.

C. S. Lewis

But this I say: He who sows sparingly will also reap sparingly, and he who sows bountifully will also reap bountifully. So let each one give as he purposes in his heart, not grudgingly or of necessity; for God loves a cheerful giver.

2 Corinthians 9:6-7 NKJV

Generosity Now

The thread of generosity is woven—completely and inextricably—into the very fabric of Christ's teachings. As He sent His disciples out to heal the sick and spread God's message of salvation, Jesus offered this guiding principle: "Freely you have received, freely give. (Matthew 10:8 NIV). The principle still applies. If we are to be disciples of Christ, we must give freely of our time, our possessions, and our love.

In 2 Corinthians 9, Paul reminds us that when we sow the seeds of generosity, we reap bountiful rewards in accordance with God's plan for our lives. Thus, we are instructed to give cheerfully and without reservation. So today, make this pledge and keep it: Be a cheerful, generous, courageous giver. The world needs your help, and you need the spiritual rewards that will be yours when you give it.

More Great Ideas About Generosity

The measure of a life, after all, is not its duration but its donation.

Corrie ten Boom

Here lies the tremendous mystery—that God should be all-powerful, yet refuse to coerce. He summons us to cooperation. We are honored in being given the opportunity to participate in His good deeds. Remember how He asked for help in performing His miracles: Fill the water pots, stretch out your hand, distribute the loaves.

Elisabeth Elliot

What is your focus today? Joy comes when it is Jesus first, others second . . . then you.

Kay Arthur

When somebody needs a helping hand, he doesn't need it tomorrow or the next day. He needs it now, and that's exactly when you should offer to help. Good deeds, if they are really good, happen sooner rather than later.

Marie T. Freeman

God does not supply money to satisfy our every whim and desire. His promise is to meet our needs and provide an abundance so that we can help other people.

Larry Burkett

We are never more like God than when we give.

Charles Swindoll

God does not need our money. But, you and I need the experience of giving it.

James Dobson

The happiest and most joyful people are those who give money and serve.

Dave Ramsey

Abundant living means abundant giving.

E. Stanley Jones

The mark of a Christian is that he will walk the second mile and turn the other cheek. A wise man or woman gives the extra effort, all for the glory of the Lord Jesus Christ.

John Maxwell

Should we accept only good from God and not adversity?

Job 2:10 HCSB

Learning the Art of Acceptance

If you're like most people, you like being in control. Period. You want things to happen according to your wishes and according to your timetable. But sometimes, God has other plans . . . and He always has the final word. Job understood the importance of accepting God's sovereignty in good times and bad . . . and so should you.

The American theologian Reinhold Niebuhr composed a profoundly simple verse that came to be known as the Serenity Prayer: "God, grant me the serenity to accept the things I cannot change, the courage to change the things I can, and the wisdom to know the difference." Niebuhr's words are far easier to recite than they are to live by.

Oswald Chambers correctly observed, "Our Lord never asks us to decide for Him; He asks us to yield to Him—a very different matter." These words remind us that even when we cannot understand the workings of God, we must trust Him and accept His will.

Are you embittered by a personal tragedy that you did not deserve and cannot understand? If so, it's time to make peace with life. It's time to forgive others, and, if necessary, to forgive yourself. It's time to accept the unchangeable past, to embrace the priceless present, and to have faith in the promise of tomorrow. It's time to trust God completely. And it's time to reclaim the peace—His peace—that can and should be yours.

So if you've encountered unfortunate circumstances that are beyond your power to control, accept those circumstances . . . and trust God. When you do, you can be comforted in the knowledge that your Creator is both loving and wise, and that He understands His plans perfectly, even when you do not.

Trust the past to God's mercy,
the present to God's love,
and the future to God's providence.

—

St. Augustine

More Great Ideas About Acceptance

When we face an impossible situation, all self-reliance and self-confidence must melt away; we must be totally dependent on Him for the resources.

Anne Graham Lotz

I have held many things in my hands, and I have lost them all; but whatever I have placed in God's hands, that I still possess.

Corrie ten Boom

Acceptance says: True, this is my situation at the moment. I'll look unblinkingly at the reality of it. But, I'll also open my hands to accept willingly whatever a loving Father sends me.

Catherine Marshall

Ultimately things work out best for those who make the best of the way things work out.

Barbara Johnson

Our Lord never asks us to decide for Him; He asks us to yield to Him—a very different matter.

Oswald Chambers

But be doers of the word, and not hearers only, deceiving yourselves.

James 1:22 NKJV

Actions Speak Louder

The old saying is both familiar and true: actions speak louder than words. And as believers, we must beware: our actions should always give credence to the changes that Christ can make in the lives of those who walk with Him.

God calls upon each of us to act in accordance with His will and with respect for His commandments. If we are to be responsible believers, we must realize that it is never enough simply to hear the instructions of God; we must also live by them. And it is never enough to wait idly by while others do God's work here on earth; we, too, must act. Doing God's work is a responsibility that each of us must bear, and when we do, our loving Heavenly Father rewards our efforts with a bountiful harvest.

Do you seek God's peace and His blessings? Then obey Him. When you're faced with a difficult choice or a powerful temptation, seek God's counsel and trust the counsel He gives. Invite God into your heart and act in accordance with His commandments. When you do, you will be blessed today, and tomorrow, and forever.

More Great Ideas About Taking Action Now

Never fail to do something because you don't feel like it. Sometimes you just have to do it now, and you'll feel like it later.

Marie T. Freeman

From the very moment one feels called to act is born the strength to bear whatever horror one will feel or see. In some inexplicable way, terror loses its overwhelming power when it becomes a task that must be faced.

Emmi Bonhoeffer

A bird does not know it can fly before it uses its wings. We learn God's love in our hearts as soon as we act upon it.

Corrie ten Boom

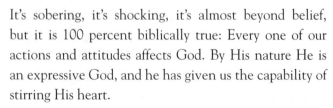

It's sobering, it's shocking, it's almost beyond belief, but it is 100 percent biblically true: Every one of our actions and attitudes affects God. By His nature He is an expressive God, and he has given us the capability of stirring His heart.

Bill Hybels

We spend our lives dreaming of the future, not realizing that a little of it slips away every day.

Barbara Johnson

We set the sail; God makes the wind.

Anonymous

Logic will not change an emotion, but action will.

Zig Ziglar

The church needs people who are doers of the Word and not just hearers.

Warren Wiersbe

Do noble things, do not dream them all day long.

Charles Kingsley

Paul did one thing. Most of us dabble in forty things. Are you a doer or a dabbler?

Vance Havner

So then, they are no longer two but one flesh. Therefore what God has joined together, let not man separate.

Matthew 19:6 NKJV

About Marriage

L ove is a journey. A healthy marriage is a lifelong exercise in love, fidelity, trust, understanding, forgiveness, caring, sharing, and encouragement. It requires empathy, tenderness, patience, and perseverance. It is the union of two adults, both of whom are willing to compromise and, when appropriate, to apologize. It requires heaping helpings of common sense, common courtesy, and uncommon caring. A healthy marriage is a joy to behold, an even greater joy to experience…and a blessing forever.

The loving relationship between a husband and wife may require the couple to travel together through the dark valleys of disappointment and sorrow, but even on those darkest days, the couple can remain steadfast . . . if they choose to follow God.

When we behave ourselves as obedient servants, we honor the Father and the Son. When we live righteously and according to God's commandments, we build better marriages and better lives. When we obey God, He blesses us in ways that we cannot fully understand. So, as this day unfolds, take every step of your journey with God as your traveling companion. Study His Holy Word. Follow His commandments. Support only those activities that further God's kingdom and your spiritual growth. Be an example of righteous living to your neighbors, to your children, and to your spouse. And make certain that you keep God where He belongs: at the center of all your relationships, including your marriage.

A marriage can't survive
forever on leftovers.
It needs to be fed continually,
or it will eventually starve.

—

John Maxwell

More Great Ideas About Marriage

Both a good marriage and a bad marriage have moments of struggle, but in a healthy relationship, the husband and wife search for answers and areas of agreement because they love each other.

James Dobson

How committed are you to breaking the ice of prayerlessness so that you and your mate can seek the Lord openly and honestly together, releasing control over your marriage into the capable, trustworthy, but often surprising hands of God?

Stormie Omartian

The institution of marriage has been a sacred bond of fidelity between a man and a woman in every culture throughout recorded history. The pledge of loyalty and mutual support represented by marriage vows is a promise of commitment that extends to every aspect of life.

James Dobson

Marriage is a divine institution, founded by God. Society did not make the first marriage; God did.

Billy Graham

Blessed are those who hunger and thirst for righteousness, because they will be filled.

Matthew 5:6 HCSB

Living Righteously

Matthew 5:6 teaches us that righteous men and women are blessed. Do you sincerely desire to be a righteous person? Are you bound and determined—despite the inevitable temptations and distractions of our modern age—to be an example of godly behavior to your family, to your friends, to your coworkers, and to your community? If so, you must obey God's commandments. There are no shortcuts and no loopholes—to be a faithful Christian, you must be an obedient Christian.

You will never become righteous by accident. You must hunger for righteousness, and you must ask God to guide your steps. When you ask Him for guidance, He will give it. So, when you're faced with a difficult choice or a powerful temptation, seek God's counsel and trust the counsel He gives. Invite God into your heart and live according to His commandments. When you do, you will be blessed today, tomorrow, and forever.

More Great Ideas About Doing What's Right

Our afflictions are designed not to break us but to bend us toward the eternal and the holy.

Barbara Johnson

Holiness has never been the driving force of the majority. It is, however, mandatory for anyone who wants to enter the kingdom.

Elisabeth Elliot

He doesn't need an abundance of words. He doesn't need a dissertation about your life. He just wants your attention. He wants your heart.

Kathy Troccoli

We have a decision to make—to turn away from sin or to be miserable and suffer the consequences of continual disobedience.

Vonette Bright

Righteousness not only defines God, but God defines righteousness.

Bill Hybels

Impurity is not just a wrong action; impurity is the state of mind and heart and soul which is just the opposite of purity and wholeness.

A. W. Tozer

Have your heart right with Christ, and he will visit you often, and so turn weekdays into Sundays, meals into sacraments, homes into temples, and earth into heaven.

C. H. Spurgeon

A man who lives right, and is right, has more power in his silence than another has by his words.

Phillips Brooks

The great thing is to be found at one's post as a child of God, living each day as though it were our last, but planning as though our world might last a hundred years.

C. S. Lewis

Becoming pure is a process of spiritual growth, and taking seriously the confession of sin during prayer time moves that process along, causing us to purge our life of practices that displease God.

Elizabeth George

Therefore humble yourselves under the mighty hand of God, that He may exalt you in due time, casting all your care upon Him, for He cares for you.

1 Peter 5:6-7 NKJV

He Cares

I t is easy to become overwhelmed by the demands of everyday life, but if you're a faithful follower of the One from Galilee, you need never be overwhelmed. Why? Because God's love is sufficient to meet your needs. Whatever dangers you may face, whatever heartbreaks you must endure, God is with you, and He stands ready to comfort you and to heal you.

The Psalmist writes, "Weeping may endure for a night, but joy comes in the morning" (Psalm 30:5 NKJV). But when we are suffering, the morning may seem very far away. It is not. God promises that He is "near to those who have a broken heart" (Psalm 34:18 NKJV).

If you are experiencing the intense pain of a recent loss, or if you are still mourning a loss from long ago, perhaps you are now ready to begin the next stage of your journey with God. If so, be mindful of this fact: the loving heart of God is sufficient to meet any challenge, including yours.

More Great Ideas About God's Support

God uses our most stumbling, faltering faith-steps as the open door to His doing for us "more than we ask or think."

Catherine Marshall

In God's faithfulness lies eternal security.

Corrie ten Boom

We have ample evidence that the Lord is able to guide. The promises cover every imaginable situation. All we need to do is to take the hand he stretches out.

Elisabeth Elliot

Snuggle in God's arms. When you are hurting, when you feel lonely or left out, let Him cradle you, comfort you, reassure you of His all-sufficient power and love.

Kay Arthur

God's help is near and always available, but it is only given to those who seek it.

Max Lucado

No matter what we are going through, no matter how long the waiting for answers, of one thing we may be sure. God is faithful. He keeps His promises. What He starts, He finishes . . . including His perfect work in us.

Gloria Gaither

We shall find in Christ enough of everything we need—for the body, for the mind, and for the spirit—to do what He wants us to do as long as He wants us to do it.

Vance Havner

How delightful a teacher, but gentle a provider, how bountiful a giver is my Father! Praise, praise to Thee, O manifested Most High.

Jim Elliot

We should learn to live in the presence of the living God. He should be a well for us: delightful, comforting, unfailing, springing up to eternal life (John 4:14). When we rely on other people, their water supplies ultimately dry up. But, the well of the Creator never fails to nourish us.

C. H. Spurgeon

In the same way faith, if it doesn't have works, is dead by itself.

James 2:17 HCSB

Faith Without Works Doesn't Work

The central message of James' letter is the need for believers to act upon their beliefs. James' instruction is clear: "faith without works is dead." We are saved by our faith in Christ, but salvation does not signal the end of our earthly responsibilities; it marks the true beginning of our work for the Lord.

If your faith in God is strong, you will find yourself drawn toward God's work. You will serve Him, not just with words or prayers, but also with deeds. Because of your faith, you will feel compelled to do God's work—to do it gladly, faithfully, joyfully, and consistently.

Today, redouble your efforts to do God's bidding here on earth. Never have the needs—or the opportunities—been greater.

More Great Ideas About Good Works

The religion of Jesus Christ has an ethical as well as a doctrinal side.

Lottie Moon

We are saved by faith alone, but faith is never alone.

John Calvin

Where there are no good works, there is no faith. If works and love do not blossom forth, it is not genuine faith, the Gospel has not yet gained a foothold, and Christ is not yet rightly known.

Martin Luther

It is faith that saves us, not works, but the faith that saves us always produces works.

C. H. Spurgeon

Those who make religion consist altogether in good works overlook the fact that works themselves are not acceptable to God unless they proceed from faith. For without faith, it is impossible to please Him. And those who make religion consist altogether in faith overlook the fact that true faith always works by love, and invariably produces the works of love.

Charles Finney

Heaven and earth will pass away, but My words will never pass away.

Matthew 24:35 HCSB

Trust God's Word

Are you a person who trusts God's Word without reservation? Hopefully so, because the Bible is unlike any other book—it is a guidebook for life here on earth and for life eternal.

As a Christian, you are instructed to study God's Holy Word, to trust His Word, to follow its commandments, and to share its Good News with the world. The Psalmist writes, "Your word is a lamp to my feet and a light to my path" (Psalm 119:105 NASB). Is the Bible your lamp? If not, you are depriving yourself of a priceless gift from the Creator.

Vance Havner observed, "It takes calm, thoughtful, prayerful meditation on the Word to extract its deepest nourishment." How true. God's Word can be a roadmap to a place of righteousness and abundance. Make it your roadmap. God's wisdom can be a light to guide your steps. Claim it as your light today, tomorrow, and every day of your life—and then walk confidently in the footsteps of God's only begotten Son.

More Great Ideas About God's Word

The Bible became a living book and a guide for my life.

Vonette Bright

For whatever life holds for you and your family in the coming days, weave the unfailing fabric of God's Word through your heart and mind. It will hold strong, even if the rest of life unravels.

Gigi Graham Tchividjian

Words fail to express my love for this holy Book, my gratitude for its author, for His love and goodness. How shall I thank him for it?

Lottie Moon

God can see clearly no matter how dark or foggy the night is. Trust His Word to guide you safely home.

Lisa Whelchel

I believe the reason so many are failing today is that they have not disciplined themselves to read God's Word consistently, day in and day out, and to apply it to every situation in life.

Kay Arthur

The promises of Scripture are not mere pious hopes or sanctified guesses. They are more than sentimental words to be printed on decorated cards for Sunday School children. They are eternal verities. They are true. There is no perhaps about them.

Peter Marshall

It takes calm, thoughtful, prayerful meditation on the Word to extract its deepest nourishment.

Vance Havner

God has given us all sorts of counsel and direction in his written Word; thank God, we have it written down in black and white.

John Eldredge

Help me, Lord, to be a student of Your Word, that I might be a better servant in Your world.

Jim Gallery

Meditating upon His Word will inevitably bring peace of mind, strength of purpose, and power for living.

Bill Bright

Acquire wisdom—how much better it is than gold! And acquire understanding—it is preferable to silver.

Proverbs 16:16 HCSB

Acquiring Wisdom

Proverbs 16:16 teaches us that wisdom is more valuable than gold. All of us would like to be wise, but not all of us are willing to do the work that is required to become wise. Wisdom is not like a mushroom; it does not spring up overnight. It is, instead, like an oak tree that starts as a tiny acorn, grows into a sapling, and eventually reaches up to the sky, tall and strong.

To become wise, we must seek God's wisdom and live according to His Word. To become wise, we must seek wisdom with consistency and purpose. To become wise, we must not only learn the lessons of the Christian life, we must also live by them.

Do you seek to live a life of righteousness and wisdom? If so, you must study the ultimate source of wisdom: the Word of God. You must seek out worthy mentors and listen carefully to their advice. You must associate, day in and day out, with godly men and women. Then, as you accumulate wisdom, you must not keep it for yourself; you must, instead, share it with your friends and family members.

But be forewarned: if you sincerely seek to share your hard-earned wisdom with others, your actions must give credence to your words. The best way to share one's wisdom—perhaps the only way—is not by words, but by example.

Knowledge is horizontal.
Wisdom is vertical;
it comes down from above.

—

Billy Graham

More Great Ideas About Wisdom

If we neglect the Bible, we cannot expect to benefit from the wisdom and direction that result from knowing God's Word.

Vonette Bright

Knowledge can be found in books or in school. Wisdom, on the other hand, starts with God . . . and ends there.

Marie T. Freeman

Wisdom is knowledge applied. Head knowledge is useless on the battlefield. Knowledge stamped on the heart makes one wise.

Beth Moore

When you and I are related to Jesus Christ, our strength and wisdom and peace and joy and love and hope may run out, but His life rushes in to keep us filled to the brim. We are showered with blessings, not because of anything we have or have not done, but simply because of Him.

Anne Graham Lotz

This is my song through endless ages: Jesus led me all the way.

Fanny Crosby

When I was a child, I spoke as a child, I understood as a child, I thought as a child; but when I became a man, I put away childish things.

1 Corinthians 13:11 NKJV

Still Growing Up

The journey toward spiritual maturity lasts a lifetime. As Christians, we can and should continue to grow in the love and the knowledge of our Savior as long as we live. Norman Vincent Peale had the following advice for believers of all ages: "Ask the God who made you to keep remaking you." That advice, of course, is perfectly sound, but often ignored.

When we cease to grow, either emotionally or spiritually, we do ourselves a profound disservice. But, if we study God's Word, if we obey His commandments, and if we live in the center of His will, we will not be "stagnant" believers; we will, instead, be growing Christians . . . and that's exactly what God intends for us to be.

Life is a series of choices and decisions. Each day, we make countless decisions that can bring us closer to God . . . or not. When we live according to the principles contained in God's Holy Word, we embark upon a journey of spiritual maturity that results in life abundant and life eternal.

More Great Ideas About Maturity

The disappointment has come, not because God desires to hurt you or make you miserable or to demoralize you, or ruin your life, or keep you from ever knowing happiness. He wants you to be perfect and complete in every aspect, lacking nothing. It's not the easy times that make you more like Jesus, but the hard times.

Kay Arthur

Salvation is the process that's done, that's secure, that no one can take away from you. Sanctification is the lifelong process of being changed from one degree of glory to the next, growing in Christ, putting away the old, taking on the new.

Max Lucado

Growth in depth and strength and consistency and fruitfulness and ultimately in Christlikeness is only possible when the winds of life are contrary to personal comfort.

Anne Graham Lotz

Integrity and maturity are two character traits vital to the heart of a leader.

Charles Stanley

I've never met anyone who became instantly mature. It's a painstaking process that God takes us through, and it includes such things as waiting, failing, losing, and being misunderstood—each calling for extra doses of perseverance.

Charles Swindoll

Being a Christian means accepting the terms of creation, accepting God as our maker and redeemer, and growing day by day into an increasingly glorious creature in Christ, developing joy, experiencing love, maturing in peace.

Eugene Peterson

We cannot hope to reach Christian maturity in any way other than by yielding ourselves utterly and willingly to His mighty working.

Hannah Whitall Smith

When I was young I was sure of everything; in a few years, having been mistaken a thousand times, I was not half so sure of most things as I was before; at present, I am hardly sure of anything but what God has revealed to me.

John Wesley

Shepherd God's flock among you, not overseeing out of compulsion but freely, according to God's will; not for the money but eagerly.

1 Peter 5:2 HCSB

Christ-Centered Leadership

The old saying is familiar and true: imitation is the sincerest form of flattery. As believers, we are called to imitate, as best we can, the carpenter from Galilee. The task of imitating Christ is often difficult and sometimes impossible, but as Christians, we must continue to try.

Our world needs leaders who willingly honor Christ with their words and their deeds, but not necessarily in that order. If you seek to be such a leader, then you must begin by making yourself a worthy example to your family, to your friends, to your church, and to your community. After all, your words of instruction will never ring true unless you yourself are willing to follow them.

Christ-centered leadership is an exercise in service: service to God in heaven and service to His children here on earth. Christ willingly became a servant to His followers, and you must seek to do the same for yours.

Are you the kind of servant-leader whom you would want to follow? If so, congratulations: you are honoring your Savior by imitating Him. And that, of course, is the sincerest form of flattery.

More Great Ideas About Leadership

You can never separate a leader's actions from his character.

John Maxwell

A man ought to live so that everybody knows he is a Christian, and most of all, his family ought to know.

D. L. Moody

A wise leader chooses a variety of gifted individuals. He complements his strengths.

Charles Stanley

What do we Christians chiefly value in our leaders? The answer seems to be not their holiness, but their gifts and skills and resources. The thought that only holy people are likely to be spiritually useful does not loom large in our minds.

J. I. Packer

All bitterness, anger and wrath, insult and slander must be removed from you, along with all wickedness. And be kind and compassionate to one another, forgiving one another, just as God also forgave you in Christ.

Ephesians 4:31-32 HCSB

Beyond Bitterness

In the fourth chapter of Ephesians, we are warned about the dangers of bitterness, and with good reason. Bitterness is a spiritual sickness. It will consume your soul; it is dangerous to your emotional health. It can destroy you if you let it . . . so don't let it!

If you are caught up in intense feelings of anger or resentment, you know all too well the destructive power of these emotions. How can you rid yourself of these feelings? First, you must prayerfully ask God to cleanse your heart. Then, you must learn to catch yourself whenever thoughts of bitterness or hatred begin to attack you. Your challenge is this: You must learn to resist negative thoughts before they hijack your emotions.

When you learn to direct your thoughts toward more positive (and rational) topics, you'll be protected from the spiritual and emotional consequences of bitterness . . . and you'll be wiser, healthier, and happier, too. So why wait? Defeat destructive bitterness today.

More Great Ideas About Bitterness

Grudges are like hand grenades; it is wise to release them before they destroy you.

Barbara Johnson

Bitterness is a spiritual cancer, a rapidly growing malignancy that can consume your life. Bitterness cannot be ignored but must be healed at the very core, and only Christ can heal bitterness.

Beth Moore

Sin is any deed or memory that hampers or binds human personality.

Catherine Marshall

Forgiveness is the key that unlocks the door of resentment and the handcuffs of hate. It is a power that breaks the chains of bitterness and the shackles of selfishness.

Corrie ten Boom

Bitterness is the trap that snares the hunter.

Max Lucado

Forgiveness enables you to bury your grudge in icy earth. To put the past behind you. To flush resentment away by being the first to forgive. Forgiveness fashions your future. It is a brave and brash thing to do.

Barbara Johnson

Bitterness only makes suffering worse and closes the spiritual channels through which God can pour His grace.

Warren Wiersbe

Bitterness is the greatest barrier to friendship with God.

Rick Warren

Be patient and understanding. Life is too short to be vengeful or malicious.

Phillips Brooks

A heart out of tune, out of sync with God's heart, will produce a life of spiritual barrenness and missed opportunities.

Jim Cymbala

Be strong and courageous, and do the work. Do not be afraid or discouraged, for the Lord God, my God, is with you.

1 Chronicles 28:20 NIV

Beyond the Fear of Failure

As we consider the uncertainties of the future, we are confronted with a powerful temptation: the temptation to "play it safe." Unwilling to move mountains, we fret over molehills. Unwilling to entertain great hopes for the tomorrow, we focus on the unfairness of the today. Unwilling to trust God completely, we take timid half-steps when God intends that we make giant leaps.

Today, ask God for the courage to step beyond the boundaries of your doubts. Ask Him to guide you to a place where you can realize your full potential—a place where you are freed from the fear of failure. Ask Him to do His part, and promise Him that you will do your part. Don't ask Him to lead you to a "safe" place; ask Him to lead you to the "right" place . . . and remember: those two places are seldom the same.

More Great Ideas About
the Fear of Failure

There comes a time when we simply have to face the challenges in our lives and stop backing down.

John Eldredge

With each new experience of letting God be in control, we gain courage and reinforcement for daring to do it again and again.

Gloria Gaither

Risk must be taken because the greatest hazard in life is to risk nothing.

John Maxwell

Do not be one of those who, rather than risk failure, never attempt anything.

Thomas Merton

Only a person who dares to risk is free.

Joey Johnson

The one who lives with integrity lives securely, but whoever perverts his ways will be found out.

Proverbs 10:9 HCSB

Integrity Matters

Charles Swindoll correctly observed, "Nothing speaks louder or more powerfully than a life of integrity." Godly men and women agree.

Integrity is built slowly over a lifetime. It is the sum of every right decision and every honest word. It is forged on the anvil of honorable work and polished by the twin virtues of honesty and fairness. Integrity is a precious thing—difficult to build but easy to tear down.

As believers in Christ, we must seek to live each day with discipline, honesty, and faith. When we do, at least two things happen: integrity becomes a habit, and God blesses us because of our obedience to Him.

Living a life of integrity isn't always the easiest way, but it is always the right way. God clearly intends that it should be our way, too.

Oswald Chambers, the author of the Christian classic devotional text, *My Utmost for His Highest*, advised, "Never support an experience which does not have God as its source, and faith in God as its result." These words serve as a powerful reminder that, as Christians, we are called to walk with God and obey His commandments. But, we live in a world that presents us with countless temptations to stray far from God's path. We Christians, when confronted with sins of any kind, have clear instructions: Walk—or better yet run—in the opposite direction.

It has been said that character is what we are when nobody is watching. How true. When we do things that we know aren't right, we try to hide them from our families and friends. But even if we successfully conceal our sins from the world, we can never conceal our sins from God.

If you sincerely wish to walk with your Creator, follow His commandments. When you do, your character will take care of itself . . . and you won't need to look over your shoulder to see who, besides God, is watching.

> Maintaining your integrity
> in a world of sham is
> no small accomplishment.

Wayne Oates

More Great Ideas About Integrity

God never called us to naïveté. He called us to integrity. The biblical concept of integrity emphasizes mature innocence not childlike ignorance.

Beth Moore

Integrity is the glue that holds our way of life together. We must constantly strive to keep our integrity intact. When wealth is lost, nothing is lost; when health is lost, something is lost; when character is lost, all is lost.

Billy Graham

Honesty has a beautiful and refreshing simplicity about it. No ulterior motives. No hidden meanings. As honesty and integrity characterize our lives, there will be no need to manipulate others.

Charles Swindoll

The single most important element in any human relationship is honesty—with oneself, with God, and with others.

Catherine Marshall

Integrity is not a given factor in everyone's life. It is a result of self-discipline, inner trust, and a decision to be relentlessly honest in all situations in our lives.

John Maxwell

There's nothing like the power of integrity. It is a characteristic so radiant, so steady, so consistent, so beautiful, that it makes a permanent picture in our minds.

Franklin Graham

The commandment of absolute truthfulness is really only another name for the fullness of discipleship.

Dietrich Bonhoeffer

You cannot glorify Christ and practice deception at the same time.

Warren Wiersbe

God doesn't expect you to be perfect, but he does insist on complete honesty.

Rick Warren

One thing I do, forgetting those things which are behind and reaching forward to those things which are ahead, I press toward the goal for the prize of the upward call of God in Christ Jesus.

Philippians 3:13-14 NKJV

Making Peace with Your Past

Because you are human, you may be slow to forget yesterday's disappointments. But, if you sincerely seek to focus your hopes and energies on the future, then you must find ways to accept the past, no matter how difficult it may be to do so.

In the third chapter of Philippians, Paul tells us that he chose to focus on the future, not the past. Have you made peace with your past? If so, congratulations. But, if you are mired in the quicksand of regret, it's time to plan your escape. How can you do so? By accepting what has been and by trusting God for what will be.

So, if you have not yet made peace with the past, today is the day to declare an end to all hostilities. When you do, you can then turn your thoughts to wondrous promises of God and to the glorious future that He has in store for you.

More Great Ideas About the Past

We can't just put our pasts behind us. We've got to put our pasts in front of God.

Beth Moore

Yesterday is just experience but tomorrow is glistening with purpose—and today is the channel leading from one to the other.

Barbara Johnson

Yesterday ended last night.

John Maxwell

Whoever you are, whatever your condition or circumstance, whatever your past or problem, Jesus can restore you to wholeness.

Anne Graham Lotz

We set our eyes on the finish line, forgetting the past, and straining toward the mark of spiritual maturity and fruitfulness.

Vonette Bright

The pages of your past cannot be rewritten, but the pages of your tomorrows are blank.

Zig Ziglar

Our yesterdays present irreparable things to us; it is true that we have lost opportunities which will never return, but God can transform this destructive anxiety into a constructive thoughtfulness for the future. Let the past sleep, but let it sleep on the bosom of Christ. Leave the Irreparable Past in His hands, and step out into the Irresistible Future with Him.

Oswald Chambers

The wise man gives proper appreciation in his life to his past. He learns to sift the sawdust of heritage in order to find the nuggets that make the current moment have any meaning.

Grady Nutt

Don't let yesterday use up too much of today.

Dennis Swanberg

Therefore, get your minds ready for action, being self-disciplined, and set your hope completely on the grace to be brought to you at the revelation of Jesus Christ.

1 Peter 1:13 HCSB

The Need for Self-Discipline

God's Word reminds us again and again that our Creator expects us to lead disciplined lives. God doesn't reward laziness, misbehavior, or apathy. To the contrary, He expects us to behave with dignity and discipline. But ours is a world in which dignity and discipline are often in short supply.

We live in a world in which leisure is glorified and indifference is often glamorized. But God has other plans. God gives us talents, and He expects us to use them. But it is not always easy to cultivate those talents. Sometimes, we must invest countless hours (or, in some cases, many years) honing our skills. And that's perfectly okay with God, because He understands that self-discipline is a blessing, not a burden.

Proverbs 23:12 advises: "Apply your heart to discipline And your ears to words of knowledge" (NASB). And, 2 Peter 1:5-6 teaches, "make every effort to supplement your faith with goodness, goodness with knowledge, knowledge with self-control, self-control with endurance, endurance with godliness" (HCSB). Thus, God's Word is clear: we must exercise self-discipline in all matters.

When we pause to consider how much work needs to be done, we realize that self-discipline is not simply a proven way to get ahead, it's also an integral part of God's plan for our lives. If we genuinely seek to be faithful stewards of our time, our talents, and our resources, we must adopt a disciplined approach to life. Otherwise, our talents are wasted and our resources are squandered.

Life's greatest rewards seldom fall into our laps; to the contrary, our greatest accomplishments usually require work, perseverance, and discipline. May we, as disciplined believers, be willing to work for the rewards we so earnestly desire.

Discipline is training that
develops and corrects.

—

Charles Stanley

More from God's Word

"They that sow bountifully shall reap also bountifully," is as true in spiritual things as in material.

Lottie Moon

Obedience to God is our job. The results of that obedience are God's.

Elisabeth Elliot

You can't climb the ladder of life with your hands in your pockets.

Barbara Johnson

As we make an offering of our work, we find the truth of a principle Jesus taught: Fulfillment is not a goal to achieve, but always the by-product of a sacrifice.

Elisabeth Elliot

Simply stated, self-discipline is obedience to God's Word and willingness to submit everything in life to His will, for His ultimate glory.

John MacArthur

The one who conceals his sins will not prosper, but whoever confesses and renounces them will find mercy.

Proverbs 28:13 HCSB

Making a Mistake

Everybody makes mistakes, and so will you. In fact, Winston Churchill once observed, "Success is going from failure to failure without loss of enthusiasm." What was good for Churchill is also good for you. You should expect to make mistakes—plenty of mistakes—but you should not allow those missteps to rob you of the enthusiasm you need to fulfill God's plan for your life.

We are imperfect people living in an imperfect world; mistakes are simply part of the price we pay for being here. But, even though mistakes are an inevitable part of life's journey, repeated mistakes should not be. When we commit the inevitable blunders of life, we must correct them, learn from them, and pray for the wisdom not to repeat them. When we do, our mistakes become lessons, and our lives become adventures in growth, not stagnation.

Have you made a mistake or three? Of course you have. But here's the big question: have you used your mistakes as stumbling blocks or stepping stones? The answer to that question will determine how well you will perform in the workplace and in every other aspect of your life.

There is nothing wrong with
asking God's direction.
But it is wrong to go our own way,
then expect Him to bail us out.

—

Larry Burkett

More Great Ideas About Mistakes

Sin is largely a matter of mistaken priorities. Any sin in us that is cherished, hidden, and not confessed will cut the nerve center of our faith.

Catherine Marshall

God is able to take mistakes, when they are committed to Him, and make of them something for our good and for His glory.

Ruth Bell Graham

Very few things motivate us to give God our undivided attention like being faced with the negative consequences of our decisions.

Charles Stanley

Mistakes offer the possibility for redemption and a new start in God's kingdom. No matter what you're guilty of, God can restore your innocence.

Barbara Johnson

In essence, my testimony is that there is life after failure: abundant, effective, spirit-filled life for those who are willing to repent hard and work hard.

Beth Moore

Commit your activities to the Lord and your plans will be achieved.

Proverbs 16:3 HCSB

Defining Success

How do you define success? Do you define it as the accumulation of material possessions or the adulation of your neighbors? If so, you need to reorder your priorities. Genuine success has little to do with fame or fortune; it has everything to do with God's gift of love and His promise of salvation.

If you have accepted Christ as your personal Savior, you are already a towering success in the eyes of God, but there is still more that you can do. Your task—as a believer who has been touched by the Creator's grace—is to accept the spiritual abundance and peace that He offers through the person of His Son. Then, you can share the healing message of God's love and His abundance with a world that desperately needs both. When you do, you will have reached the pinnacle of success.

More Great Ideas About Success

Winners see an answer for every problem; losers see a problem in every answer.

Barbara Johnson

In essence, my testimony is that there is life after failure: abundant, effective, spirit-filled life for those who are willing to repent hard and work hard.

Beth Moore

There's not much you can't achieve or endure if you know God is walking by your side. Just remember: Someone knows, and Someone cares.

Bill Hybels

We, as believers, must allow God to define success. And, when we do, God blesses us with His love and His grace.

Jim Gallery

Success or failure can be pretty well predicted by the degree to which the heart is fully in it.

John Eldredge

God provides the ingredients for our daily bread but expects us to do the baking. With our own hands!

Barbara Johnson

Maintenance of the devotional mood is indispensable to success in the Christian life.

A. W. Tozer

Often, attitude is the only difference between success and failure.

John Maxwell

Success isn't the key. Faithfulness is.

Joni Eareckson Tada

Victory is the result of Christ's life lived out in the believer. It is important to see that victory, not defeat, is God's purpose for His children.

Corrie ten Boom

Success and happiness are not destinations. They are exciting, never-ending journeys.

Zig Ziglar

Do not be deceived: "Bad company corrupts good morals."

1 Corinthians 15:33 HCSB

Following God, Not "The Crowd"

Rick Warren observed, "Those who follow the crowd usually get lost in it." We know those words to be true, but oftentimes we fail to live by them. Instead of trusting God for guidance, we imitate our friends and suffer the consequences. Instead of seeking to please our Father in heaven, we strive to please our peers, with decidedly mixed results. Instead of doing the right thing, we do the "easy" thing or the "popular" thing. And when we do, we pay a high price for our shortsightedness.

Would you like a time-tested formula for successful living? Here is a simple formula that is proven and true: don't give in to peer pressure. Period.

Instead of getting lost in the crowd, you should find guidance from God. Does this sound too simple? Perhaps it is simple, but it is also the only way to reap all the marvelous riches that God has in store for you.

More Great Ideas About Peer Pressure

For better or worse, you will eventually become more and more like the people you associate with. So why not associate with people who make you better, not worse?

Marie T. Freeman

It is comfortable to know that we are responsible to God and not to man. It is a small matter to be judged of man's judgement.

Lottie Moon

We, as God's people, are not only to stay far away from sin and sinners who would entice us, but we are to be so like our God that we mourn over sin.

Kay Arthur

You will get untold flak for prioritizing God's revealed and present will for your life over man's . . . but, boy, is it worth it.

Beth Moore

Do you want to be wise? Choose wise friends.

Charles Swindoll

Fashion is an enduring testimony to the fact that we live quite consciously before the eyes of others.

John Eldredge

Those who follow the crowd usually get lost in it.

Rick Warren

Comparison is the root of all feelings of inferiority.

James Dobson

It's tempting to follow the crowd, but usually it's better to follow your conscience.

Criswell Freeman

Ambition! We must be careful what we mean by it. If it means the desire to get ahead of other people—which is what I think it does mean—then it is bad. If it simply means wanting to do a thing well, then it is good. It isn't wrong for an actor to want to act his part as well as it can possibly be acted, but the wish to have his name in bigger type than the other actors is a bad one.

C. S. Lewis

So he who had received five talents came and brought five other talents, saying, "Lord, you delivered to me five talents; look, I have gained five more talents besides them." His lord said to him, "Well done, good and faithful servant; you were faithful over a few things, I will make you ruler over many things. Enter into the joy of your lord."

Matthew 25:20-21 NKJV

Using Your Talents

The old saying is both familiar and true: "What we are is God's gift to us; what we become is our gift to God." Each of us possesses special talents, gifted by God, that can be nurtured carefully or ignored totally. Our challenge, of course, is to use our abilities to the greatest extent possible and to use them in ways that honor our Savior.

Are you using your natural talents to make God's world a better place? If so, congratulations. But if you have gifts that you have not fully explored and developed, perhaps you need to have a chat with the One who gave you those gifts in the first place. Your talents are priceless treasures offered from your Heavenly Father. Use them. After all, an obvious way to say "thank you" to the Giver is to use the gifts He has given.

More Great Ideas About Talents

Not everyone possesses boundless energy or a conspicuous talent. We are not equally blessed with great intellect or physical beauty or emotional strength. But we have all been given the same ability to be faithful.

Gigi Graham Tchividjian

What we are is God's gift to us. What we become is our gift to God.

Anonymous

In the great orchestra we call life, you have an instrument and a song, and you owe it to God to play them both sublimely.

Max Lucado

God has given you special talents—now it's your turn to give them back to God.

Marie T. Freeman

You are the only person on earth who can use your ability.

Zig Ziglar

God often reveals His direction for our lives through the way He made us . . . with a certain personality and unique skills.

Bill Hybels

You are a unique blend of talents, skills, and gifts, which makes you an indispensable member of the body of Christ.

Charles Stanley

One thing taught large in the Holy Scriptures is that while God gives His gifts freely, He will require a strict accounting of them at the end of the road. Each man is personally responsible for his store, be it large or small, and will be required to explain his use of it before the judgment seat of Christ.

A. W. Tozer

The Lord is glad to open the gate to every knocking soul. It opens very freely; its hinges are not rusted, no bolts secure it. Have faith and enter at this moment through holy courage. If you knock with a heavy heart, you shall yet sing with joy of spirit. Never be discouraged!

C. H. Spurgeon

My cup runs over. Surely goodness and mercy shall follow me all the days of my life; and I will dwell in the house of the Lord Forever.

Psalm 23:5-6 NKJV

Optimistic Christianity

Pessimism and Christianity don't mix. Why? Because Christians have every reason to be optimistic about life here on earth and life eternal. As C. H. Spurgeon observed, "Our hope in Christ for the future is the mainstream of our joy." But sometimes, we fall prey to worry, frustration, anxiety, or sheer exhaustion, and our hearts become heavy. What's needed is plenty of rest, a large dose of perspective, and God's healing touch, but not necessarily in that order.

Today, make this promise to yourself and keep it: vow to be a hope-filled Christian. Think optimistically about your life, your profession, your future, and your family. Trust your hopes, not your fears. Take time to celebrate God's glorious creation. And then, when you've filled your heart with hope and gladness, share your optimism with others. They'll be better for it, and so will you. But not necessarily in that order.

More Great Ideas About Optimism

Christ can put a spring in your step and a thrill in your heart. Optimism and cheerfulness are products of knowing Christ.

Billy Graham

The Christian lifestyle is not one of legalistic do's and don'ts, but one that is positive, attractive, and joyful.

Vonette Bright

The popular idea of faith is of a certain obstinate optimism: the hope, tenaciously held in the face of trouble, that the universe is fundamentally friendly and things may get better.

J. I. Packer

The essence of optimism is that it takes no account of the present, but it is a source of inspiration, of vitality, and of hope. Where others have resigned, it enables a man to hold his head high, to claim the future for himself, and not abandon it to his enemy.

Dietrich Bonhoeffer

The people whom I have seen succeed best in life have always been cheerful and hopeful people who went about their business with a smile on their faces.

Charles Kingsley

Developing a positive attitude means working continually to find what is uplifting and encouraging.

Barbara Johnson

Keep your feet on the ground, but let your heart soar as high as it will. Refuse to be average or to surrender to the chill of your spiritual environment.

A. W. Tozer

If our hearts have been attuned to God through an abiding faith in Christ, the result will be joyous optimism and good cheer.

Billy Graham

It is a remarkable thing that some of the most optimistic and enthusiastic people you will meet are those who have been through intense suffering.

Warren Wiersbe

Rejoice in hope; be patient in affliction; be persistent in prayer.

Romans 12:12 HCSB

The Power of Patience

Most of us are impatient for God to grant us the desires of our heart. Usually, we know what we want, and we know precisely when we want it: right now, if not sooner. But God may have other plans. And when God's plans differ from our own, we must trust in His infinite wisdom and in His infinite love.

As busy men and women living in a fast-paced world, many of us find that waiting quietly for God is difficult. Why? Because we are fallible human beings seeking to live according to our own timetables, not God's. In our better moments, we realize that patience is not only a virtue, but it is also a commandment from God.

God instructs us to be patient in all things. We must be patient with our families, our friends, and our associates. We must also be patient with our Creator as He unfolds His plan for our lives. And that's as it should be. After all, think how patient God has been with us.

More Great Ideas About Patience

Waiting is the hardest kind of work, but God knows best, and we may joyfully leave all in His hands.

Lottie Moon

God is more patient with us than we are with ourselves.

Max Lucado

If God is diligent, surely we ought to be diligent in doing our duty to Him. Think how patient and diligent God has been to us!

Oswald Chambers

When I am dealing with an all-powerful, all-knowing God, I, as a mere mortal, must offer my petitions not only with persistence, but also with patience. Someday I'll know why.

Ruth Bell Graham

In the Bible, patience is not a passive acceptance of circumstances. It is a courageous perseverance in the face of suffering and difficulty.

Warren Wiersbe

The next time you're disappointed, don't panic. Don't give up. Just be patient and let God remind you he's still in control.

Max Lucado

Grass that is here today and gone tomorrow does not require much time to mature. A big oak tree that lasts for generations requires much more time to grow and mature. God is concerned about your life through eternity. Allow Him to take all the time He needs to shape you for His purposes. Larger assignments will require longer periods of preparation.

Henry Blackaby

When we read of the great Biblical leaders, we see that it was not uncommon for God to ask them to wait, not just a day or two, but for years, until God was ready for them to act.

Gloria Gaither

It is wise to wait because God gives clear direction only when we are willing to wait.

Charles Stanley

Do you not know that the runners in a stadium all race, but only one receives the prize? Run in such a way that you may win. Now everyone who competes exercises self-control in everything. However, they do it to receive a perishable crown, but we an imperishable one.

1 Corinthians 9:24-25 HCSB

The Power of Perseverance

In a world filled with roadblocks and stumbling blocks, we need strength, courage, and perseverance. And, as an example of perfect perseverance, we need look no further than our Savior, Jesus Christ.

Jesus finished what He began. Despite the torture He endured, despite the shame of the cross, Jesus was steadfast in His faithfulness to God. We, too, must remain faithful, especially during times of hardship.

Perhaps you are in a hurry for God to reveal His plans for your life. If so, be forewarned: God operates on His own timetable, not yours. Sometimes, God may answer your prayers with silence, and when He does, you must patiently persevere. In times of trouble, you must remain steadfast and trust in the merciful goodness of your Heavenly Father. Whatever your problem, He can handle it.

More Great Ideas About Perseverance

Battles are won in the trenches, in the grit and grime of courageous determination; they are won day by day in the arena of life.

Charles Swindoll

If things are tough, remember that every flower that ever bloomed had to go through a whole lot of dirt to get there.

Barbara Johnson

You cannot persevere unless there is a trial in your life. There can be no victories without battles; there can be no peaks without valleys. If you want the blessing, you must be prepared to carry the burden and fight the battle. God has to balance privileges with responsibilities, blessings with burdens, or else you and I will become spoiled, pampered children.

Warren Wiersbe

Perseverance is more than endurance. It is endurance combined with absolute assurance and certainty that what we are looking for is going to happen.

Oswald Chambers

Only the man who follows the command of Jesus single-mindedly and unresistingly lets his yoke rest upon him, finds his burden easy, and under its gentle pressure receives the power to persevere in the right way.

Dietrich Bonhoeffer

Failure is one of life's most powerful teachers. How we handle our failures determines whether we're going to simply "get by" in life or "press on."

Beth Moore

By perseverance the snail reached the ark.

C. H. Spurgeon

Are you a Christian? If you are, how can you be hopeless? Are you so depressed by the greatness of your problems that you have given up all hope? Instead of giving up, would you patiently endure? Would you focus on Christ until you are so preoccupied with him alone that you fall prostrate before him?

Anne Graham Lotz

We are all on our way somewhere. We'll get there if we just keep going.

Barbara Johnson

Therefore, as we have opportunity, we must work for the good of all, especially for those who belong to the household of faith.

Galatians 6:10 HCSB

Today's Opportunities

Are you excited about the opportunities of today and thrilled by the possibilities of tomorrow? Do you confidently expect God to lead you to a place of abundance, peace, and joy? And, when your days on earth are over, do you expect to receive the priceless gift of eternal life? If you trust God's promises, and if you have welcomed God's Son into your heart, then you believe that your future is intensely and eternally bright.

Today, as you prepare to meet the duties of everyday life, pause and consider God's promises. And then think for a moment about the wonderful future that awaits all believers, including you. God has promised that your future is secure. Trust that promise, and celebrate the life of abundance and eternal joy that is now yours through Christ.

More Great Ideas About Opportunities

He who waits until circumstances completely favor his undertaking will never accomplish anything.

Martin Luther

God surrounds you with opportunity. You and I are free in Jesus Christ, not to do whatever we want, but to be all that God wants us to be.

Warren Wiersbe

Great opportunities often disguise themselves in small tasks.

Rick Warren

We are all faced with a series of great opportunities, brilliantly disguised as unsolvable problems. Unsolvable without God's wisdom, that is.

Charles Swindoll

Life is a glorious opportunity.

Billy Graham

Winners see an answer for every problem; losers see a problem in every answer.

Barbara Johnson

Listen, my son, to your father's instruction and do not forsake your mother's teaching.

Proverbs 1:8 NIV

Keep Learning

When it comes to learning life's lessons, we can either do things the easy way or the hard way. The easy way can be summed up as follows: when God teaches us a lesson, we learn it . . . the first time! Unfortunately, too many of us learn much more slowly than that.

When we resist our Heavenly Father's instruction, He continues to teach, whether we like it or not. Our challenge, then, is to discern God's lessons from the experiences of everyday life. Hopefully, we learn those lessons sooner rather than later because the sooner we do, the sooner He can move on to the next lesson and the next, and the next . . .

It's the things you learn
after you know it all
that really count.

—

Vance Havner

More Great Ideas About Learning

God is able to take mistakes, when they are committed to Him, and make of them something for our good and for His glory.

Ruth Bell Graham

While chastening is always difficult, if we look to God for the lesson we should learn, we will see spiritual fruit.

Vonette Bright

True learning can take place at every age of life, and it doesn't have to be in the curriculum plan.

Suzanne Dale Ezell

Our loving God uses difficulty in our lives to burn away the sin of self and build faith and spiritual power.

Bill Bright

The wonderful thing about God's schoolroom is that we get to grade our own papers. You see, He doesn't test us so He can learn how well we're doing. He tests us so we can discover how well we're doing.

Charles Swindoll

For if you forgive people their wrongdoing, your heavenly Father will forgive you as well. But if you don't forgive people, your Father will not forgive your wrongdoing.

Matthew 6:14-15 HCSB

Forgiveness Now

Forgiving other people is hard—sometimes very hard. But God tells us that we must forgive others, even when we'd rather not. So, if you're angry with anybody (or if you're upset by something you yourself have done), it's time to forgive . . . now!

Life would be much simpler if you could forgive people "once and for all" and be done with it. Yet forgiveness is seldom that easy. Usually, the decision to forgive is straightforward, but the process of forgiving is more difficult. Forgiveness is a journey that requires effort, time, perseverance, and prayer.

God instructs you to treat other people exactly as you wish to be treated. And since you want to be forgiven for the mistakes that you make, you must be willing to extend forgiveness to other people for the mistakes that they have made. If you can't seem to forgive someone, you should keep asking God to help you until you can. You can be sure of this: if you keep asking for God's help, He will give it.

More Great Ideas About Forgiveness

As you have received the mercy of God by the forgiveness of sin and the promise of eternal life, thus you must show mercy.

Billy Graham

Only the truly forgiven are truly forgiving.

C. S. Lewis

Our relationships with other people are of primary importance to God. Because God is love, He cannot tolerate any unforgiveness or hardness in us toward any individual.

Catherine Marshall

Forgiveness is not an emotion. Forgiveness is an act of the will, and the will can function regardless of the temperature of the heart.

Corrie ten Boom

Revenge is the raging fire that consumes the arsonist.

Max Lucado

The more you practice the art of forgiving, the quicker you'll master the art of living.

Marie T. Freeman

Our forgiveness toward others should flow from a realization and appreciation of God's forgiveness toward us.

Franklin Graham

To hold on to hate and resentments is to throw a monkey wrench into the machinery of life.

E. Stanley Jones

I firmly believe a great many prayers are not answered because we are not willing to forgive someone.

D. L. Moody

It is better to forgive and forget than to resent and remember.

Barbara Johnson

A merry heart does good, like medicine.

Proverbs 17:22 NKJV

Cheerfulness Is a Gift

Cheerfulness is a gift that we give to others and to ourselves. And, as believers who have been saved by a risen Christ, why shouldn't we be cheerful? The answer, of course, is that we have every reason to honor our Savior with joy in our hearts, smiles on our faces, and words of celebration on our lips.

Few things in life are more sad, or, for that matter, more absurd, than grumpy Christians. Christ promises us lives of abundance and joy if we accept His love and His grace. Yet sometimes, even the most righteous among us are beset by fits of ill temper and frustration. During these moments, we may not feel like turning our thoughts and prayers to Christ, but if we seek to gain perspective and peace, that's precisely what we must do.

Are you a cheerful Christian? You should be! And what is the best way to attain the joy that is rightfully yours? By giving Christ what is rightfully His: your heart, your soul, and your life.

More Great Ideas About Cheerfulness

The people whom I have seen succeed best in life have always been cheerful and hopeful people who went about their business with a smile on their faces.

Charles Kingsley

God is good, and heaven is forever. And if those two facts don't cheer you up, nothing will.

Marie T. Freeman

Sour godliness is the devil's religion.

John Wesley

We may run, walk, stumble, drive, or fly, but let us never lose sight of the reason for the journey, or miss a chance to see a rainbow on the way.

Gloria Gaither

Christ can put a spring in your step and a thrill in your heart. Optimism and cheerfulness are products of knowing Christ.

Billy Graham

Be anxious for nothing, but in everything by prayer and supplication, with thanksgiving, let your requests be made known to God.

Philippians 4:6 NKJV

Beyond Anxiety

We live in a world that often breeds anxiety and fear. When we come face to face with tough times, we may fall prey to discouragement, doubt, or depression. But our Father in Heaven has other plans. God has promised that we may lead lives of abundance, not anxiety. In fact, His Word instructs us to "be anxious for nothing." But how can we put our fears to rest? By taking those fears to God and leaving them there.

As you face the challenges of everyday living, do you find yourself becoming anxious, troubled, discouraged, or fearful? If so, turn every one of your concerns over to your Heavenly Father. The same God who created the universe will comfort you if you ask Him...so ask Him and trust Him. And then watch in amazement as your anxieties melt into the warmth of His loving hands.

Worry and anxiety are sand
in the machinery of life;
faith is the oil.

—

E. Stanley Jones

More Great Ideas About
Anxiety

Some people feel guilty about their anxieties and regard them as a defect of faith, but they are afflictions, not sins. Like all afflictions, they are, if we can so take them, our share in the passion of Christ.

C. S. Lewis

So often we pray and then fret anxiously, waiting for God to hurry up and do something. All the while God is waiting for us to calm down, so He can do something through us.

Corrie ten Boom

We must lay our questions, frustrations, anxieties, and impotence at the feet of God and wait for His answer. And then receiving it, we must live by faith.

Kay Arthur

The fierce grip of panic need not immobilize you. God knows no limitation when it comes to deliverance. Admit your fear. Commit it to Him. Dump the pressure on Him. He can handle it.

Charles Swindoll

Don't be deceived: God is not mocked. For whatever a man sows he will also reap, because the one who sows to his flesh will reap corruption from the flesh, but the one who sows to the Spirit will reap eternal life from the Spirit.

Galatians 6:7-8 HCSB

Choose Wisely

L ife is a series of choices. Each day, we make countless decisions that can bring us closer to God… or not. When we live according to God's commandments, we earn for ourselves the abundance and peace that He intends for our lives. But, when we turn our backs upon God by disobeying Him, we bring needless suffering upon ourselves and our families.

Do you seek God's peace and His blessings? Then obey Him. When you're faced with a difficult choice or a powerful temptation, seek God's counsel and trust the counsel He gives. Invite God into your heart and live according to His commandments. When you do, you will be blessed today, and tomorrow, and forever.

More Great Ideas About Behavior

Don't worry about what you do not understand. Worry about what you do understand in the Bible but do not live by.

Corrie ten Boom

Our response to God determines His response to us.

Henry Blackaby

There may be no trumpet sound or loud applause when we make a right decision, just a calm sense of resolution and peace.

Gloria Gaither

When you discover the Christian way, you discover your own way as a person.

E. Stanley Jones

Christianity says we were created by a righteous God to flourish and be exhilarated in a righteous environment. God has "wired" us in such a way that the more righteous we are, the more we'll actually enjoy life.

Bill Hybels

Then He said to Thomas, "Put your finger here and observe My hands. Reach out your hand and put it into My side. Don't be an unbeliever, but a believer."

John 20:27 HCSB

Actions and Beliefs

Our theology must be demonstrated, not only by our words but, more importantly, by our actions. As Christians, we must do our best to make sure that our actions are accurate reflections of our beliefs. In short, we should be practical believers, quick to act whenever we see an opportunity to serve God.

We may proclaim our beliefs to our hearts' content, but our proclamations will mean nothing—to others or to ourselves—unless we accompany our words with deeds that match. The sermons that we live are far more compelling than the ones we preach. So remember this: whether you like it or not, your life is an accurate reflection of your creed. If this fact gives you cause for concern, don't bother talking about the changes that you intend to make—make them. And then, when your good deeds speak for themselves—as they most certainly will—don't interrupt.

More Great Ideas About Belief

What I believe about God is the most important thing about me.

A. W. Tozer

The reason many of us do not ardently believe in the gospel is that we have never given it a rigorous testing, thrown our hard questions at it, or faced it with our most prickly doubts.

Eugene Peterson

I believe in Christ as I believe in that the Sun has risen, not only because I see it, but because by it I see everything else.

C. S. Lewis

The mind is a faculty, and magnificent one at that. But the heart is the dwelling place of our true beliefs.

John Eldredge

What we believe determines how we behave, and both determine what we become.

Warren Wiersbe

The Lord bless you and keep you; the Lord make His face shine upon you, and be gracious to you.

Numbers 6:24-25 NKJV

Counting Your Blessings

If you sat down and began counting your blessings, how long would it take? A very, very long time! Your blessings include life, freedom, family, friends, talents, and possessions, for starters. But, your greatest blessing—a gift that is yours for the asking—is God's gift of salvation through Christ Jesus.

Today, begin making a list of your blessings. You most certainly will not be able to make a complete list, but take a few moments and jot down as many blessings as you can. Then give thanks to the giver of all good things: God. His love for you is eternal, as are His gifts. And it's never too soon—or too late—to offer Him thanks.

More Great Ideas About Blessings

God's kindness is not like the sunset—brilliant in its intensity, but dying every second. God's generosity keeps coming and coming and coming.

Bill Hybels

When you and I are related to Jesus Christ, our strength and wisdom and peace and joy and love and hope may run out, but His life rushes in to keep us filled to the brim. We are showered with blessings, not because of anything we have or have not done, but simply because of Him.

Anne Graham Lotz

Do we not continually pass by blessings innumerable without notice, and instead fix our eyes on what we feel to be our trials and our losses, and think and talk about these until our whole horizon is filled with them, and we almost begin to think we have no blessings at all?

Hannah Whitall Smith

God is more anxious to bestow His blessings on us than we are to receive them.

St. Augustine

God blesses us in spite of our lives and not because of our lives.

Max Lucado

Think of the blessings we so easily take for granted: Life itself; preservation from danger; every bit of health we enjoy; every hour of liberty; the ability to see, to hear, to speak, to think, and to imagine all this comes from the hand of God.

Billy Graham

Get rich quick! Count your blessings!

Anonymous

The key to a blessed life is to have a listening heart that longs to know what the Lord is saying.

Jim Cymbala

Jesus intended for us to be overwhelmed by the blessings of regular days. He said it was the reason he had come: "I am come that they might have life, and that they might have it more abundantly."

Gloria Gaither

I the Lord do not change.

Malachi 3:6 HCSB

What Doesn't Change

We live in a world that is always changing, but we worship a God that never changes—thank goodness! That means that we can be comforted in the knowledge that our Heavenly Father is the rock that simply cannot be moved.

The next time you face difficult circumstances, tough times, unfair treatment, or unwelcome changes, remember that some things never change—things like the love that you feel in your heart for your family and friends . . . and the love that God feels for you. So, instead of worrying too much about life's inevitable challenges, focus your energies on finding solutions. Have faith in your own abilities, do your best to solve your problems, and leave the rest up to God.

More Great Ideas About Change

How much of our lives are, well, so daily. How often our hours are filled with the mundane, seemingly unimportant things that have to be done, whether at home or work. These very "daily" tasks could become a celebration of praise. "It is through consecration," someone has said, "that drudgery is made divine."

Gigi Graham Tchividjian

Some of us seem so anxious about avoiding hell that we forget to celebrate our journey toward heaven.

Philip Yancey

God has a course mapped out for your life, and all the inadequacies in the world will not change His mind. He will be with you every step of the way. And though it may take time, He has a celebration planned for when you cross over the "Red Seas" of your life.

Charles Swindoll

The main joy of heaven will be the heavenly Father greeting us in a time and place of rejoicing, celebration, joy, and great reunion.

Bill Bright

In terms of the parable of the Prodigal Son, repentance is the flight home that leads to joyful celebration. It opens the way to a future, to a relationship restored.

Philip Yancey

Both a good marriage and a bad marriage have moments of struggle, but in a healthy relationship, the husband and wife search for answers and areas of agreement because they love each other.

James Dobson

The fewer words, the better prayer.

Martin Luther

But I'm convinced the best way to cope with change, ironically enough, is to get to know a God who doesn't change, One who provides an anchor in the swirling seas of change.

Bill Hybels

Part of good communication is listening with the eyes as well as with the ears.

Josh McDowell

Beloved, if God so loved us, we also ought to love one another.

1 John 4:11 NKJV

Friendship Matters

Genuine friendship should be treasured and nourished. How? The surest way is by observing the Golden Rule.

As Christians, we are governed by the Golden Rule: we are commanded to treat others as we wish to be treated. And when we treat others with kindness, courtesy, and respect, we build friendships that can last a lifetime.

Throughout the Bible, we are reminded to love one another and care for one another. In other words, the Bible teaches us that friendship is as friendship does.

Do you want to have great friends? Then be one. And make no mistake: that's exactly the kind of friend that God wants you to be.

More Great Ideas About Friends

Trust is the soil in which the flower of friendship grows.

Marie T. Freeman

In friendship, God opens your eyes to the glories of Himself.

Joni Eareckson Tada

Friendships are living organisms at work. They continue to unfold, change, and emerge.

Barbara Johnson

The glory of friendship is not the outstretched hand, or the kindly smile, or the joy of companionship. It is the spiritual inspiration that comes to one when he discovers that someone else believes in him and is willing to trust him with his friendship.

Corrie ten Boom

Yes, the Spirit was sent to be our Counselor. Yes, Jesus speaks to us personally. But often he works through another human being.

John Eldredge

Though I know intellectually how vulnerable I am to pride and power, I am the last one to know when I succumb to their seduction. That's why spiritual Lone Rangers are so dangerous—and why we must depend on trusted brothers and sisters who love us enough to tell us the truth.

Chuck Colson

Don't bypass the potential for meaningful friendships just because of differences. Explore them. Embrace them. Love them.

Luci Swindoll

I have found that the closer I am to the godly people around me, the easier it is for me to live a righteous life because they hold me accountable.

John MacArthur

True friends don't spend time gazing into each other's eyes. They show great tenderness toward each other, but they face in the same direction, toward common projects, interest, goals, and above all, toward a common Lord.

C. S. Lewis

For I know the thoughts that I think toward you, says the Lord, thoughts of peace and not of evil, to give you a future and a hope. Then you will call upon Me and go and pray to Me, and I will listen to you.

Jeremiah 29:11-12 NKJV

Your Very Bright Future

Because we are saved by a risen Christ, we can have hope for the future, no matter how troublesome our present circumstances may seem. After all, God has promised that we are His throughout eternity. And, He has told us that we must place our hopes in Him.

Of course, we will face disappointments and failures while we are here on earth, but these are only temporary defeats. This world can be a place of trials and tribulations, but when we place our trust in the Giver of all things good, we are secure. God has promised us peace, joy, and eternal life. And God keeps His promises today, tomorrow, and forever.

Are you willing to place your future in the hands of a loving and all-knowing God? Do you trust in the ultimate goodness of His plan for your life? Will you face today's challenges with optimism and hope? You should.

After all, God created you for a very important purpose: His purpose. And you still have important work to do: His work.

Today, as you live in the present and look to the future, remember that God has a plan for you. Act—and believe—accordingly.

Take courage.
We walk in the wilderness today
and in the Promised Land tomorrow.

—

D. L. Moody

More Great Ideas About Future

You can look forward with hope, because one day there will be no more separation, no more scars, and no more suffering in My Father's House. It's the home of your dreams!

Anne Graham Lotz

The future lies all before us. Shall it only be a slight advance upon what we usually do? Ought it not to be a bound, a leap forward to altitudes of endeavor and success undreamed of before?

Annie Armstrong

Every saint has a past—every sinner has a future!

Anonymous

Allow your dreams a place in your prayers and plans. God-given dreams can help you move into the future He is preparing for you.

Barbara Johnson

Don't ever forget there are more firsts to come.

Dennis Swanberg

This is how we are sure that we have come to know Him: by keeping His commands.

1 John 2:3 HCSB

Obeying His Commandments

E lisabeth Elliot advised, "Obedience to God is our job. The results of that obedience are God's." These words serve to remind us that obedience is imperative, but we live in a society that surrounds us with temptations to disobey God's laws. So if we are to win the battle against temptation and sin, we must never drop our guard.

A righteous life has many components: faith, honesty, generosity, love, kindness, humility, gratitude, and worship, to name but a few. If we seek to follow the steps of our Savior, Jesus Christ, we must seek to live according to His commandments.

When we seek righteousness in our own lives— and when we seek the companionship of likeminded friends—we not only build our characters, but we also reap the spiritual rewards that God offers those who obey Him. When we live in accordance with God's commandments, He blesses us in ways that we cannot fully understand.

Are you ready, willing, able, and anxious to receive God's blessings? Then obey Him. And rest assured that when you do your part, He'll do His part.

Don't worry about
what you do not understand.
Worry about what you do understand
in the Bible but do not live by.

—

Corrie ten Boom

More Great Ideas About God's Commandments

Only grief and disappointment can result from continued violation of the divine principles that underlie the spiritual life.

A. W. Tozer

Let us remember therefore this lesson: That to worship our God sincerely we must evermore begin by hearkening to His voice, and by giving ear to what He commands us. For if every man goes after his own way, we shall wander. We may well run, but we shall never be a whit nearer to the right way, but rather farther away from it.

John Calvin

Bible history is filled with people who began the race with great success but failed at the end because they disregarded God's rules.

Warren Wiersbe

God meant that we adjust to the Gospel—not the other way around.

Vance Havner

In all your ways acknowledge Him, and He shall direct your paths.

Proverbs 3:6 NKJV

Seeking God's Guidance

When we genuinely seek to know the heart of God—when we prayerfully seek His wisdom and His will—our Heavenly Father carefully guides us over the peaks and valleys of life. And as Christians, we can be comforted: Whether we find ourselves at the pinnacle of the mountain or the darkest depths of the valley, the loving heart of God is always there with us.

As Christians whose salvation has been purchased by the blood of Christ, we have every reason to live joyously and courageously. After all, Christ has already fought and won our battle for us—He did so on the cross at Calvary. But despite Christ's sacrifice, and despite God's promises, we may become confused or disoriented by the endless complications and countless distractions of modern life.

If you're unsure of your next step, lean upon God's promises and lift your prayers to Him. Remember that God is always near; remember that He is your protector and your deliverer. Open yourself to His heart, and trust Him to guide your path. When you do, God will direct your steps, and you will receive His blessings today, tomorrow, and throughout eternity.

More Great Ideas About God's Guidance

Are you serious about wanting God's guidance to become a personal reality in your life? The first step is to tell God that you know you can't manage your own life; that you need his help.

Catherine Marshall

If we want to hear God's voice, we must surrender our minds and hearts to Him.

Billy Graham

Walk in the daylight of God's will because then you will be safe; you will not stumble.

Anne Graham Lotz

It is a joy that God never abandons His children. He guides faithfully all who listen to His directions.

Corrie ten Boom

A man's heart plans his way, but the Lord directs his steps.

Proverbs 16:9 NKJV

His Plans for You

God has a plan for your life. He understands that plan as thoroughly and completely as He knows you. And, if you seek God's will earnestly and prayerfully, He will make His plans known to you in His own time and in His own way.

If you sincerely seek to live in accordance with God's will for your life, you will live in accordance with His commandments. You will study God's Word, and you will be watchful for His signs.

Sometimes, God's plans seem unmistakably clear to you. But other times, He may lead you through the wilderness before He directs you to the Promised Land. So be patient and keep seeking His will for your life. When you do, you'll be amazed at the marvelous things that an all-powerful, all-knowing God can do.

More Great Ideas About God's Plan

God has a plan for the life of every Christian. Every circumstance, every turn of destiny, all things work together for your good and for His glory.

Billy Graham

If not a sparrow falls upon the ground without your Father, you have reason to see that the smallest events of your career and your life are arranged by him.

C. H. Spurgeon

If you believe in a God who controls the big things, you have to believe in a God who controls the little things. It is we, of course, to whom things look "little" or "big."

Elisabeth Elliot

God has a course mapped out for your life, and all the inadequacies in the world will not change His mind. He will be with you every step of the way. And though it may take time, He has a celebration planned for when you cross over the "Red Seas" of your life.

Charles Swindoll

It's incredible to realize that what we do each day has meaning in the big picture of God's plan.

Bill Hybels

Our heavenly Father never takes anything from his children unless he means to give them something better.

George Mueller

I thought God's purpose was to make me full of happiness and joy. It is, but it is happiness and joy from God's standpoint, not from mine.

Oswald Chambers

God's goal is not to make you happy. It is to make you his.

Max Lucado

I don't doubt that the Holy Spirit guides your decisions from within when you make them with the intention of pleasing God. The error would be to think that He speaks only within, whereas in reality He speaks also through Scripture, the Church, Christian friends, and books.

C. S. Lewis

Can you understand the secrets of God? His limits are higher than the heavens; you cannot reach them! They are deeper than the grave; you cannot understand them! His limits are longer than the earth and wider than the sea.

Job 11:7-9 NCV

He Reigns

God is sovereign. He reigns over the entire universe, and He reigns over your little corner of that universe. Your challenge is to recognize God's sovereignty, to live in accordance with His commandments, and to trust His promises. Sometimes, of course, these tasks are easier said than done.

Your Heavenly Father may not always reveal Himself as quickly (or as clearly) as you would like. But rest assured: God is in control, God is here, and God intends to use you in wonderful, unexpected ways. He desires to lead you along a path of His choosing. Your challenge is to watch, to listen, to learn . . . and to follow. Today.

More Great Ideas About God's Sovereignty

Nothing happens by happenstance. I am not in the hands of fate, nor am I the victim of man's whims or the devil's ploys. There is One who sits above man, above Satan, and above all heavenly hosts as the ultimate authority of all the universe. That One is my God and my Father!

Kay Arthur

We do not understand the intricate pattern of the stars in their course, but we know that He Who created them does, and that just as surely as He guides them, He is charting a safe course for us.

Billy Graham

Every experience God gives us, every person he brings into our lives, is the perfect preparation for the future that only he can see.

Corrie ten Boom

God is God. He knows what he is doing. When you can't trace his hand, trust his heart.

Max Lucado

Waiting is the hardest kind of work, but God knows best, and we may joyfully leave all in His hands.

Lottie Moon

He has the right to interrupt your life. He is Lord. When you accepted Him as Lord, you gave Him the right to help Himself to your life anytime He wants.

Henry Blackaby

As you place yourself under the sovereign lordship of Jesus Christ, each mistake or failure can lead you right back to the throne.

Barbara Johnson

You will feel that He must rule and control each day. All of life and conversation must be in the Spirit. My prayer, my faith, my fellowship with the Father, and all my work in God's service, must be completely under His sway. As the Spirit of Holiness, He is the Spirit of my sanctification.

Andrew Murray

Rejoice always, pray without ceasing, in everything give thanks; for this is the will of God in Christ Jesus for you.

1 Thessalonians 5:16-18 NKJV

Be Thankful

For most of us, life is busy and complicated. We have countless responsibilities, some of which begin before sunrise and many of which end long after sunset. Amid the rush and crush of the daily grind, it is easy to lose sight of God and His blessings. But, when we forget to slow down and say "Thank You" to our Maker, we rob ourselves of His presence, His peace, and His joy.

Our task, as believing Christians, is to praise God many times each day. Then, with gratitude in our hearts, we can face our daily duties with the perspective and power that only He can provide.

More Great Ideas About Gratitude

Gratitude unlocks the fullness of life. It turns what we have into enough, and more. It turns denial into acceptance, chaos to order, confusion to clarity. It can turn a meal into a feast, a house into a home, a stranger into a friend. Gratitude makes sense of our past, brings peace for today, and creates a vision for tomorrow.

Melody Beattie

We become happy, spiritually prosperous people not because we receive what we want, but because we appreciate what we have.

Penelope Stokes

Contentment comes when we develop an attitude of gratitude for the important things we do have in our lives that we tend to take for granted if we have our eyes staring longingly at our neighbor's stuff.

Dave Ramsey

It is only with gratitude that life becomes rich.

Dietrich Bonhoeffer

Pride goes before destruction, and a haughty spirit before a fall.

Proverbs 16:18 NKJV

Beware of Pride

The words from Proverbs 16 remind us that pride and destruction are traveling partners. But as imperfect human beings, we are tempted to puff out our chests and crow about our own accomplishments. When we do so, we delude ourselves.

As Christians, we have a profound reason to be humble: We have been refashioned and saved by Jesus Christ, and that salvation came not because of our own good works but because of God's grace. Thus, we are not "self-made"; we are "God-made" and "Christ-saved." How, then, can we be boastful? The answer, of course, is simple: if we are honest with ourselves and with our God, we cannot be boastful. In the quiet moments, when we search the depths of our own hearts, we know that whatever "it" is, God did that. And He deserves the credit.

More Great Ideas About Pride

That's what I love about serving God. In His eyes, there are no little people . . . because there are no big people. We are all on the same playing field. We all start at square one. No one has it better than the other, or possesses unfair advantage.

Joni Eareckson Tada

We cannot be filled until we are empty. We have to be poor in spirit of ourselves in order to be filled with the Holy Spirit.

Corrie ten Boom

It was as important to me that my children be no more self-righteous than they were unrighteous. In His Gospels, Christ seemed far more tolerant of a repentant sinner than a self-righteous, self-proclaimed saint.

Beth Moore

Our Lord did not say it was wrong to pray in the corners of the street, but he did say it was wrong to have the motive to "be seen of men."

Oswald Chambers

All kindness and good deeds, we must keep silent. The result will be an inner reservoir of personality power.

Catherine Marshall

There is nothing so natural to man, nothing so insidious and hidden from our sight, nothing so difficult and dangerous, as pride.

Andrew Murray

Jesus had a humble heart. If He abides in us, pride will never dominate our lives.

Billy Graham

Humility is a thing which must be genuine; the imitation of it is the nearest thing in the world to pride.

C. H. Spurgeon

When you have good, healthy relationships with your family and friends you're more prompted to laugh and not take yourself so seriously.

Dennis Swanberg

Pride has a devilish quality that keeps us from sensing our need for God's grace.

Jim Cymbala

And He told them, "Watch out and be on guard against all greed, because one's life is not in the abundance of his possessions."

Luke 12:15 HCSB

The Right Kind of Treasure

All of mankind is engaged in a colossal, worldwide treasure hunt. Some people seek treasure from earthly sources, treasures such as material wealth or public acclaim; others seek God's treasures by making Him the cornerstone of their lives.

What kind of treasure hunter are you? Are you so caught up in the demands of everyday living that you sometimes allow the search for worldly treasures to become your primary focus? If so, it's time to think long and hard about what you value, and why.

All the items on your daily to-do list are not created equal. That's why you must do the hard work of putting first things first. And the "first things" in life definitely have less to do with material riches and more to do with riches of the spiritual kind.

More Great Ideas About Materialism

If you want to be truly happy, you won't find it on an endless quest for more stuff. You'll find it in receiving God's generosity and then passing that generosity along.

Bill Hybels

The Scriptures also reveal the warning that if we are consumed with greed, not only do we disobey God, but we will miss the opportunity to allow Him to use us as instruments for others.

Charles Stanley

Here's a simple test: If you can see it, it's not going to last. The things that last are the things you cannot see.

Dennis Swanberg

The cross is laid on every Christian. It begins with the call to abandon the attachments of this world.

Dietrich Bonhoeffer

Why is love of gold more potent than love of souls?

Lottie Moon

A wise man will hear and increase learning, and a man of understanding will attain wise counsel.

Proverbs 1:5 NKJV

Finding the Right Mentors

Here's a simple yet effective way to strengthen your faith: Choose role models whose faith in God is strong.

When you emulate godly people, you become a more godly person yourself. That's why you should seek out mentors who, by their words and their presence, make you a better person and a better Christian.

Today, as a gift to yourself, select, from your friends and family members, a mentor whose judgment you trust. Then listen carefully to your mentor's advice and be willing to accept that advice, even if accepting it requires effort, or pain, or both. Consider your mentor to be God's gift to you. Thank God for that gift, and use it for the glory of His kingdom.

More Great Ideas About Mentors

God guides through the counsel of good people.

E. Stanley Jones

It takes a wise person to give good advice, but an even wiser person to take it.

Marie T. Freeman

A single word, if spoken in a friendly spirit, may be sufficient to turn one from dangerous error.

Fanny Crosby

No matter how crazy or nutty your life has seemed, God can make something strong and good out of it. He can help you grow wide branches for others to use as shelter.

Barbara Johnson

God often keeps us on the path by guiding us through the counsel of friends and trusted spiritual advisors.

Bill Hybels

Be on your guard, so that your minds are not dulled from carousing, drunkenness, and worries of life.

Luke 21:34 HCSB

The Wisdom of Moderation

Would you like to improve—dramatically improve—the quality of your life? Then here's a simple, time-tested formula: learn to harness your appetites and to restrain your impulses. In other words, learn the wisdom of moderation.

When we learn to temper our appetites, our desires, and our impulses, we are blessed, in part, because God has created a world in which temperance is rewarded and intemperance is inevitably punished.

Moderation is difficult, of course; it is especially difficult in a prosperous society such as ours. But the rewards of moderation are numerous and long-lasting. Claim those rewards today. No one can force you to moderate your appetites. The decision to live temperately (and wisely) is yours and yours alone. And so are the consequences.

More Great Ideas About Moderation

We are all created differently. We share a common need to balance the different parts of our lives.

Dr. Walt Larimore

Every moment of resistance to temptation is a victory.

Frederick William Faber

To many, total abstinence is easier than perfect moderation.

St. Augustine

Contentment has a way of quieting insatiable desires.

Mary Hunt

Begin to be now what you will be hereafter.

St. Jerome

Virtue—even attempted virtue—brings light; indulgence brings fog.

C. S. Lewis

For I am the Lord, I do not change.

Malachi 3:6 NKJV

He Does Not Change

Our world is in a state of constant change. God is not. At times, the world seems to be trembling beneath our feet. But we can be comforted in the knowledge that our Heavenly Father is the rock that cannot be shaken. His Word promises, "I am the Lord, I do not change."

Every day that we live, we mortals encounter a multitude of changes—some good, some not so good. And on occasion, all of us must endure life-changing personal losses that leave us heartbroken. When we do, our Heavenly Father stands ready to comfort us, to guide us, and—in time—to heal us.

Is the world spinning a little too fast for your liking? Are you facing difficult circumstances or unwelcome changes? If so, please remember that God is far bigger than any problem you may face. So, instead of worrying about life's inevitable challenges, put your faith in the Father and His only begotten Son. After all, "Jesus Christ is the same yesterday, today, and forever" (Hebrews 13:8 NKJV). And it is precisely because your

Savior does not change that you can face your challenges with courage for today and hope for tomorrow.

Are you anxious about situations that you cannot control? Take your anxieties to God. Are you troubled? Take your troubles to Him. Does your little corner of the universe seem to be trembling beneath your feet? Seek protection from the One who cannot be moved. The same God who created the universe will protect you if you ask Him . . . so ask Him . . . and then serve Him with willing hands and a trusting heart.

God does not tell us
what He is going to do;
He reveals to us who He is.

—

Oswald Chambers

More Great Ideas About God

God can see clearly no matter how dark or foggy the night is. Trust His Word to guide you safely home.

Lisa Whelchel

We may blunder on for years thinking we know a great deal about Him, and then, perhaps suddenly, we catch a sight of Him as He is revealed in the face of Jesus Christ, and we discover the real God.

Hannah Whitall Smith

God is the beyond in the midst of our life.

Dietrich Bonhoeffer

God's actual divine essence and his will are absolutely beyond all human thought, human understanding or wisdom; in short, they are and ever will be incomprehensible, inscrutable, and altogether hidden to human reason.

Martin Luther

The God who dwells in heaven is willing to dwell also in the heart of the humble believer.

Warren Wiersbe

To God be the glory, great things He has done; / So loved He the world that He gave us His Son.

Fanny Crosby

I lived with Indians who made pots out of clay which they used for cooking. Nobody was interested in the pot. Everybody was interested in what was inside. The same clay taken out of the same riverbed, always made in the same design, nothing special about it. Well, I'm a clay pot, and let me not forget it. But, the excellency of the power is of God and not us.

Elisabeth Elliot

When we are young, change is a treat, but as we grow older, change becomes a threat. But when Jesus Christ is in control of your life, you need never fear change or decay.

Warren Wiersbe

When all else is gone, God is still left. Nothing changes Him.

Hannah Whitall Smith

God is bigger than we can figure.

Criswell Freeman

You are the light of the world. A city that is set on a hill cannot be hidden. Nor do they light a lamp and put it under a basket, but on a lampstand, and it gives light to all who are in the house. Let your light so shine before men, that they may see your good works and glorify your Father in heaven.

Matthew 5:14-16 NKJV

You Are the Light

Matthew 5:14-16 makes it clear: Because you are a Christian, you are indeed "the light of the world." The Bible also says that you should live in a way that lets other people understand what it means to be a follower of Jesus.

Your personal testimony is profoundly important, but perhaps because of shyness (or because of the fear of being rebuffed), you've been hesitant to share your experiences. If so, you should start paying less attention to your own insecurities and more attention to the message that God wants you to share with the world.

Corrie ten Boom observed, "There is nothing anybody else can do that can stop God from using us. We can turn everything into a testimony." Her words remind us that when we speak up for God, our actions may speak even more loudly than our words.

When we let other people know the details of our faith, we assume an important responsibility: the responsibility of making certain that our words are reinforced by our actions. When we share our testimonies, we must also be willing to serve as shining examples of righteousness—undeniable examples of the changes that Jesus makes in the lives of those who accept Him as their Savior.

Are you willing to follow in the footsteps of Jesus? If so, you must also be willing to talk about Him. And make no mistake—the time to express your belief in Him is now. You know how He has touched your own heart; help Him do the same for others.

In your desire to share the gospel,
you may be the only Jesus
someone else will ever meet.
Be real and be involved with people.

—

Barbara Johnson

More Great Ideas About Witnessing

There is no thrill quite as wonderful as seeing someone else come to trust Christ because I have been faithful in sharing the story of my own faith.

Vonette Bright

We must go out and live among them, manifesting the gentle, loving spirit of our Lord. We need to make friends before we can hope to make converts.

Lottie Moon

God has ordained that others may see the reality of His presence by the illumination our lives shed forth.

Beth Moore

The evangelistic harvest is always urgent. The destiny of men and of nations is always being decided. Every generation is strategic. We are not responsible for the past generation, and we cannot bear the full responsibility for the next one, but we do have our generation. God will hold us responsible as to how well we fulfill our responsibilities to this age and take advantage of our opportunities.

Billy Graham

Stay on the issue of Christ when witnessing, not the church, or denominations, or religion, or theological differences, or doctrinal questions. Speak precisely of Jesus, the Savior.

Charles Swindoll

Every tiny bit of my life that has value I owe to the redemption of Jesus Christ. Am I doing anything to enable Him to bring His redemption into evident reality in the lives of others?

Oswald Chambers

Jesus' images portray the Kingdom as a kind of secret force. Sheep among wolves, treasure hidden in a field, the tiniest seed in a garden, wheat growing among weeds, a pinch of yeast worked into bread dough; all these hint at a movement that works within society, changing it from the inside out.

Philip Yancey

When Christians live out their faith with authenticity and boldness, they put a little zing into a sometimes bland cup of soup. They catch people off guard and make them wince. They wake people up with their challenges and seemingly radical points of view. And, they overturn a few applecarts here and there.

Bill Hybels

I was glad when they said unto me, let us go into the house of the LORD.

Psalm 122:1 KJV

Our Need to Worship God

All of humanity is engaged in worship. The question is not whether we worship, but what we worship. Wise men and women choose to worship God. When they do, they are blessed with a plentiful harvest of joy, peace, and abundance. Other people choose to distance themselves from God by foolishly worshiping things that are intended to bring personal gratification but not spiritual gratification. Such choices often have tragic consequences.

If we place our love for material possessions above our love for God—or if we yield to the countless temptations of this world—we find ourselves engaged in a struggle between good and evil, a clash between God and Satan. Our responses to these struggles have implications that echo throughout our families and throughout our communities.

How can we ensure that we cast our lot with God? We do so, in part, by the practice of regular, purposeful worship in the company of fellow believers. When we worship God faithfully and fervently, we are blessed. When we fail to worship God, for whatever reason, we forfeit the spiritual gifts that He intends for us.

We must worship our Heavenly Father, not just with our words, but also with deeds. We must honor Him, praise Him, and obey Him. As we seek to find purpose and meaning for our lives, we must first seek His purpose and His will. For believers, God comes first. Always first.

Do you place a high value on the practice of worship? Hopefully so. After all, every day provides countless opportunities to put God where He belongs: at the very center of your life. It's up to you to worship God seven days a week; anything less is simply not enough.

Spiritual worship is focusing all we are on all He is.

—

Beth Moore

More Great Ideas About Worship

In the sanctuary, we discover beauty: the beauty of His presence.

Kay Arthur

God has promised to give you all of eternity. The least you can do is give Him one day a week in return.

Marie T. Freeman

In Biblical worship you do not find the repetition of a phrase; instead, you find the worshipers rehearsing the character of God and His ways, reminding Him of His faithfulness and His wonderful promises.

Kay Arthur

God actually delights in and pursues our worship (Proverbs 15:8 & John 4:23).

Shirley Dobson

To worship Him in truth means to worship Him honestly, without hypocrisy, standing open and transparent before Him.

Anne Graham Lotz

I am of the opinion that we should not be concerned about working for God until we have learned the meaning and delight of worshipping Him.

A. W. Tozer

When God is at the center of your life, you worship. When he's not, you worry.

Rick Warren

Each time, before you intercede, be quiet first and worship God in His glory. Think of what He can do and how He delights to hear the prayers of His redeemed people. Think of your place and privilege in Christ, and expect great things!

Andrew Murray

Worship is spiritual. Our worship must be more than just outward expression, it must also take place in our spirits.

Franklin Graham

Inside the human heart is an undeniable, spiritual instinct to commune with its Creator.

Jim Cymbala